CW00551178

SHADOW TYPE

CLASSIC THREE-DIM

SHADO

STEVEN HELLER

Thames & Hudson

NSIONAL LETTERING

W TYPE

AND LOUISE FILI

STEVEN HELLER is the co-chair of the MFA Design program at the School of Visual Arts, New York, and the "Visuals" columnist for *The New York Times Book Review*. He is the author, editor and co-author of over 150 books, including fifteen with Louise Fili.

LOUISE FILI is the principal of Louise Fili Ltd, a New York City-based design firm specializing in restaurant identities and food packaging. The author of *Elegantissima*, she was inducted into the Art Directors Club Hall of Fame in 2004.

First published in the United Kingdom in 2013 by Thames & Hudson Ltd,
181A High Holborn, London WC1V 7QX

Book design by Spencer Charles/Louise Fili Ltd
Cover design by Louise Fili and Spencer Charles
All images from the collection of Steven Heller and Louise Fili

British Library Cataloguing-in-Publication Data
A catalogue record for this book is available from the British Library
ISBN 978-0-500-51699-7

Printed and bound in Malaysia by C. S. Graphics

CONTENTS

INTRODUCTION

"TYPOGRAPHY CRACKED THE VOICES OF SILENCE," MARSHALL McLuhan famously wrote in *Gutenberg Galaxy: The Making of Typographic Man* (1962). Following Gutenberg's invention of the printing press, "the human voice closed down," McLuhan continues. "People began to read silently and passively... Architecture and sculpture dried up too. In literature only people from backward oral areas had any resonance to inject into the language."

Come on, Professor M! Can typography really be to blame? With its many styles and variations, typography has contributed more to communications than any other discovery, with perhaps the notable exception of the prehistoric paintings in the caves at Lascaux, La Marche, and Niaux. The mass production of the printed word may have prompted a decline in oral narrative traditions, yet the extraordinary accessibility of print has both increased and enhanced other forms of storytelling. Different typefaces have injected words with expression, emotion, and—let's not forget—dimension.

Dimensional typefaces have made all kinds of stories more visible. Contrary to McLuhan's claim, in the case of dimensional lettering, the type was not designed for solitary reading or quiet contemplation. Shadow faces tend to be loud and bold because if you capture the attention of the eye, the mind will follow. Noisy, demonstrative letters were designed to make an impression with their exaggerated scale, shape, and ornament.

"It was the nineteenth-century printer who was first confronted with this demand on his skill," writes Canadian typographer Carl Dair in *Design With Type* (1982). "He turned to strong display and decoration as a means of attracting attention to the message. Highly decorative types and ornaments were cut to meet the demand for something new and different; printers competed among themselves to see how many different typefaces could be jammed into the setting of a single message; type founders cut large wood type, hoping that sheer size would overpower the reader; compositors outdid themselves in bending and twisting their rules and type lines, only to produce a typographic wreckage."

In the commercial environment, an increasing demand for decoration produced a wide range of shadow types. Designers and craftsmen used wood, metal, and glass to craft unique typefaces to sell their products. As Dair explains, the results "found a ready sale among the newly rich merchants and members of the industrial class" who wanted to advertise their businesses to the general public. Shadows were more than mere graphic tricks; they were also veritable signposts of consumption.

The genesis of shadow letters is not entirely obscured. They can be found in the liturgical manuscripts of the Middle Ages (albeit in very elaborate forms). They make occasional appearances on late 18th-century merchants' signs. Come the early 19th century, shadows begin to proliferate in the hand-drawn iterations of both classical and newly invented type styles. The notable type founders Vincent Figgins, William Thorowgood, and John Stephenson popularized many of the most lasting letterforms, which were introduced as metal typefaces as early as 1815. The shadow did not become a conventional feature of printed text until later on in the 19th century, however, when it became essential for businesses to compete with each other by displaying their wares on posters and bills. These signs and adverts, on both urban and rural buildings, employed dimensional lettering for greater clarity.

Many shadow styles started out as Fat Faces with thin stems and hair serifs that often proved difficult to reproduce on conventional presses. Type founders compensated by adding dimensional devices to the more troublesome cuts and they were pleased with the surprisingly illusionary results. "It is as if the designers were absorbed in enjoying the ingenuity of their own invention," writes type historian Nicolete Gray in *Nineteenth Century Ornamented Typefaces* (1976). The new designs were soon adopted by commercial printers, since whatever their size, the typefaces seemed to jump off the page.

Following a surge in the popularity of shadow type among printers and their clients, type foundries began to publish books with generous selections of styles and sizes—some rather awkward concoctions, others curiously elegant. For example, novelist and playwright Honoré de Balzac, proprietor of his own foundry in Paris, issued a lavish catalog of specimens, which included a varied assortment of "*Lettres Égyptiennes Ombrées*"—heavy slab serif types with linear dimensional shading. Shadow wood type was also in demand in the late 19th century; it came in extra-large sizes so could be used outdoors to seize the eye of the frantic passer-by. Whether custom drawn, or as metal or wood type, shadow letters animated newspaper and magazine mastheads, product labels, and, indeed, all kinds of signs and posters.

Dimensional typefaces toy with human perceptions, challenging the limits of cognition. Whether framed by a subtle tint or bold silhouette, in color or in black and white, a shadow adds bulk, enabling words to rise voluminously from otherwise flat and unmonumental surfaces. Shadow faces are typographic *trompes l'œil*, facsimiles of real three-dimensional letters and inscriptions in sculpture and architecture that are dramatized by the numerous ways in which natural or artificial light falls upon them. The sun, for instance, can increase or decrease the depth of a shadow as it rises and sets, distorting both the shape and proportions of the shaded area. This sculptural essence of shadow type adds not only to the letters' visibility, but also to their continuing allure.

In the beginning sign painters mimicked sculpted letterforms, adding depth to letters on glass, wood, canvas, enameled metal, or, in fact, any acceptable surface. Subsequently, although shadow type is often found on a small scale in printed pages and on posters, some of the finest—indeed most colorful—examples of dimensional lettering are much larger, appearing on late 19th- to mid-20th-century store windows and on glass or enamel merchants' signs. Created by hand with incredible precision, these shadow letters were the virtual precursors of illumination before the invention of neon lighting in the early 20th century and effective substitutes for electronic lettering long afterward. Depending on the intensity of the artificial light source, hue of the silhouette, and color of the background on which they sat, the words were often as radiant as their neon counterparts. Years of hard-earned skill were needed to make the shadows work so as not to overcomplicate the lettering.

The golden age of shadow type ran from the late 19th to the mid-20th century, and yet this dynamic letterform has never become entirely passé. A well-composed stack of luminescent shadow letters on a poster is still as aesthetically satisfying as a beautifully designed piece of furniture. During the heyday of dimensional lettering, typographic trends and branding styles did not fluctuate as often as they do now. As businesses were not as quick to update their publicity, shadow type was more integrated into the overall vernacular of commercial art. However, like hemlines, shadows have increased or decreased depending on the fashion. As graphic styles evolved over the years, from heavy Victorian scripts to efflorescent Art Nouveau swirls to more subtle Art Deco curves, the nature of the shadow changed as well. It was with only the more restrained designs of the Bauhaus in 1920s Germany, and later with the typefaces invented in Switzerland after the Second World War, that drop shadows came to be considered as decorative indulgences.

The examples collected here date from the turn of the century to the 1950s. There are specimens from the 1930s, signaling a streamlined ethos, while 1940s scripts express a noir sensibility. The 1950s experienced a revival of more traditional lettering, with the new typefaces essentially being copies of earlier designs. In the 1960s, with the continuing interest in Victorian, Art Nouveau, and Art Deco styles and the transfiguration of these vintage letterforms into psychedelic youth graphics, shadow letters returned in full flower. Today, dimensional lettering is just another option in the type designer's toolkit. For us, however, this elegant type style still casts a long and exciting shadow.

AMERICAN

DIMENSIONAL TYPE EMERGED IN THE UNITED STATES DURING the Second Industrial Revolution in the latter half of the 19th century. Where there was industry, there were products to be advertised. Every available printable or paintable space on which letters could appear was used to sell consumption. Subsequently, a unique venue for outdoor advertising that required the boldest of typefaces was popularized in the United States over the course of the century: the billboard. An American institution, it has its roots in the large signs painted on the sides of barns and other roadside buildings. With such limited time to transmit a message, words could not be too long, and strong gothics and shadow letters were employed to ensure visibility. Color was also used to create a lasting impression.

In *American Wood Type: 1828–1900* (1969), Rob Roy Kelly highlights the importance of a particular genre of wood-type printing to the 19th-century American advertising industry. "Chromatic types," he says, "were made to print in two or more colors. These types, produced in register as corresponding pairs, were designed so that one color would overlap another in certain places to create a third color." Striking multicolored styles appeared frequently in the foundry type catalogs of the 1840s and '50s. "The high point of Chromatic wood type production," Kelly writes, "came in 1874 when the William H. Page Wood Type Co. issued their 100-page *Specimens of Chromatic Type & Borders*." Wood type is three-dimensional, so designing new styles was as easy as shining a light on the typecase and copying the directions of the shadows below.

The American shadow never really fell out of favor, although it was more popular in certain periods than in others. Advertising was the field in which dimensional lettering was most widely adopted, with loud typefaces adding volume to the shouting matches between never-ending crowds of street signs and bills. Significantly, the shadow became a symbol of power and affluence as shaded letters were used just as frequently on banknotes, stock certificates, and official documents as on product labels and brand logos. Like the massive concrete edifices of the banks and industry buildings constructed during the Second Industrial Revolution, heavy dimensional type epitomized American might in all its various forms.

BURDOCK BLOOD BITTERS

1892

B.B.B.

ALMANAC AND KEY TO HEALTH

FOSTER, MILBURN & Co. BUFFALO, N.Y.

NELLIE McHENRY
AS THE
INDIAN PRINCESS.
NATE SALSBURY
AS
The TRAGEDIAN.

ury's

OUBADOURS

IN Green Room · FUN ·

ON HOWARD'S · SUCCESSFUL · MUSICAL ····

· NOVELTY · in 3 ACTS ····

G the ADVENTURES of a PARTY OF AMATURES

ESSED With a DESIRE for a ····

SE BEHIND the SCENES OF a THEATRE"

PAL

PATENT TRANS

FOR GLASS, W

MANUF

THE PALM

INCORP

FACTORY:

Nuremberg, Bavaria.

Gener

15

HAM

CINCIN

M'S

FER LETTERS

OD,
DAINT,
in METAL
&C.

RED.

Y-

ETTER CO.

ATED.

Offices
17=.
ND ST.,
I, OHIO.

BRANCH OFFICES:
Paris, London & Vienna.

AF
MR
WL

F J N P T U
V W Y
V Y
T W
U
10
T V W Y
A
10
T V W Y
A
F P T V W Y
10
T V W Y
A
10
T V W Y
A J U
10
V Y
T U W
J
N P T U
E
V W Y
V
Y
W
T
U
C
G O Q
20

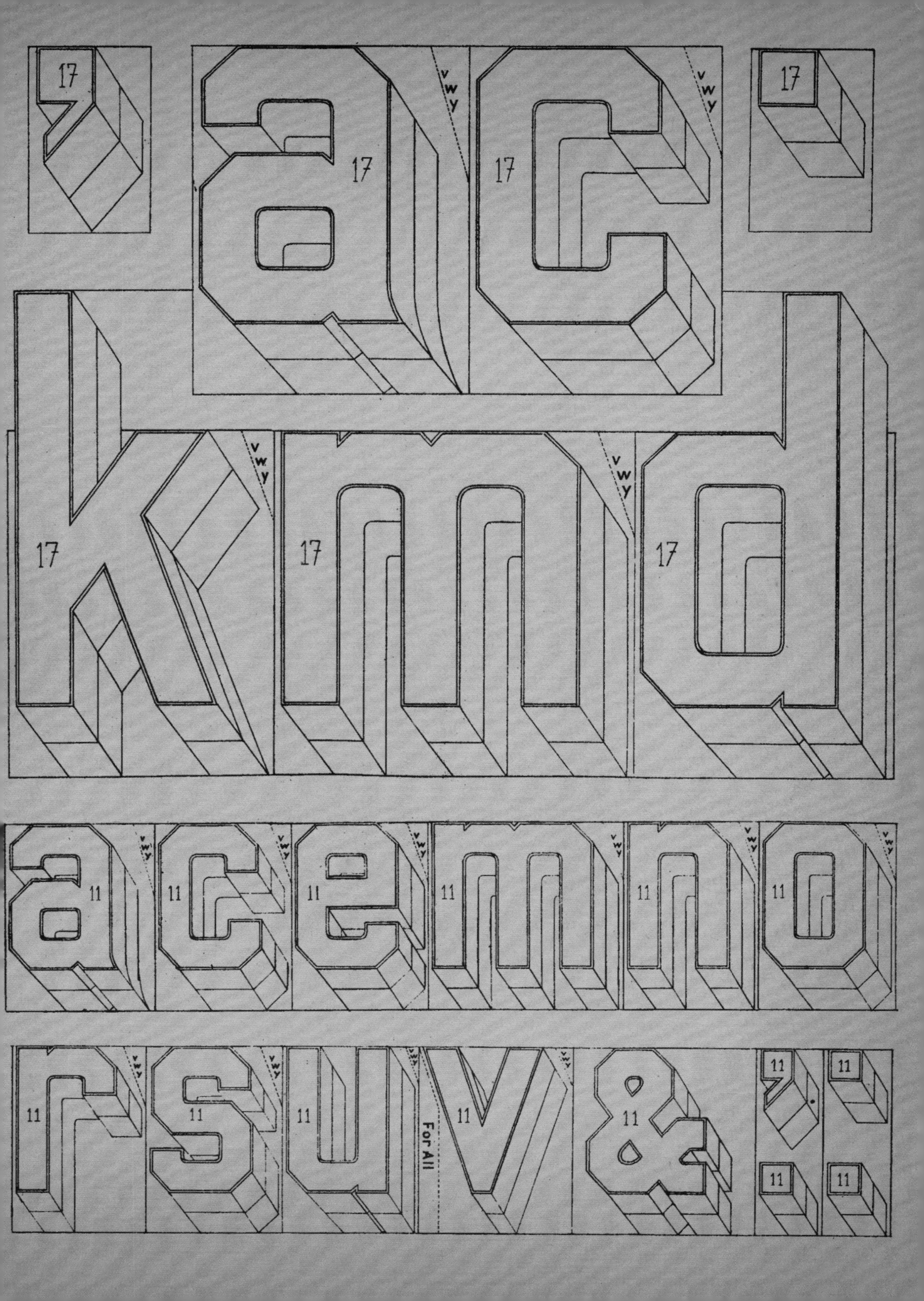
17
v w y
11
For All

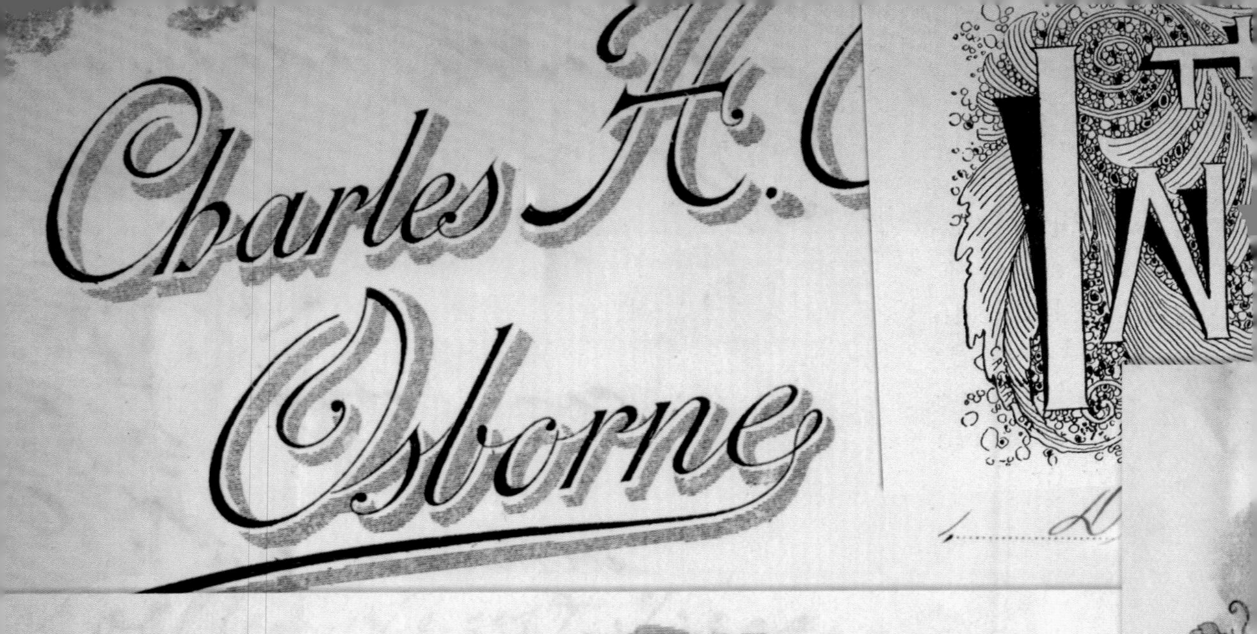

H.M. Sanders Co.
PAINTS AND OILS

MARTIN A. METZNER
YOUNG & METZNER
SUCCESSORS TO
PETER YOUNG
Bags and Bagging
SUGAR BAG CLOTH
FOR COVERING COTTON.
NEW YORK CITY.
BOROUGH OF QUEENS.
LONG ISLAND CITY, N
CAMDEN, N.J.
Long Island City, N.Y. Oct-1-1900

AND PRINTER

Thomas Henry & Son's,
DEALERS IN
TIOGA MILLS
COTTON
AND
Cotton Waste,
& MANUFACTURERS OF
ress:-

OFFICE OF
DR. DAVID KENNEDY,
NO GOODS SENT C.O.D.
PHYSICIAN & SURGEON
PROPRIETOR OF
DR. DAVID KENNEDY'S
FAVORITE REMEDY.
SALT RHEUM CREAM.
ROSE JELLY.
MAGIC EYE SALVE.
GOLDEN DROPS
WORM SYRUP
GOLDEN PLASTERS

CHERRY BALSAM.

ILLUSTRATED
MME. DEMORESTS
THE

MONTHLY.
BER.
ROR OF FASHIONS.
NSERVATOR
OF THE
Useful
TAINING AND
TIFUL

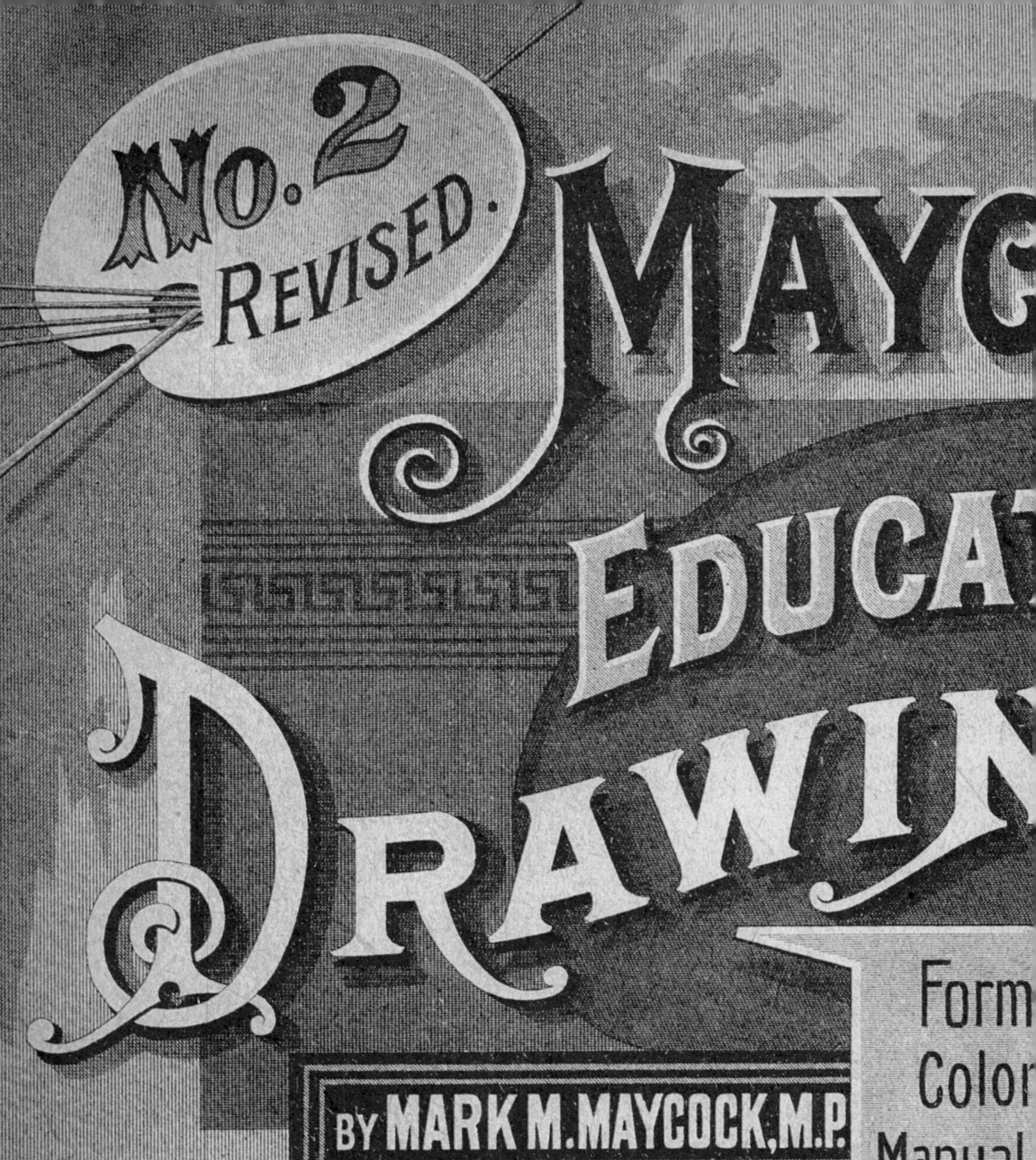

OTTO ULBRICH,
PUBLISHER.

OCK'S

IONAL

G BOOK

udy,
udy,
ining
wing.

State Normal School, Buffalo, N.Y.

BUFFALO, N.Y.

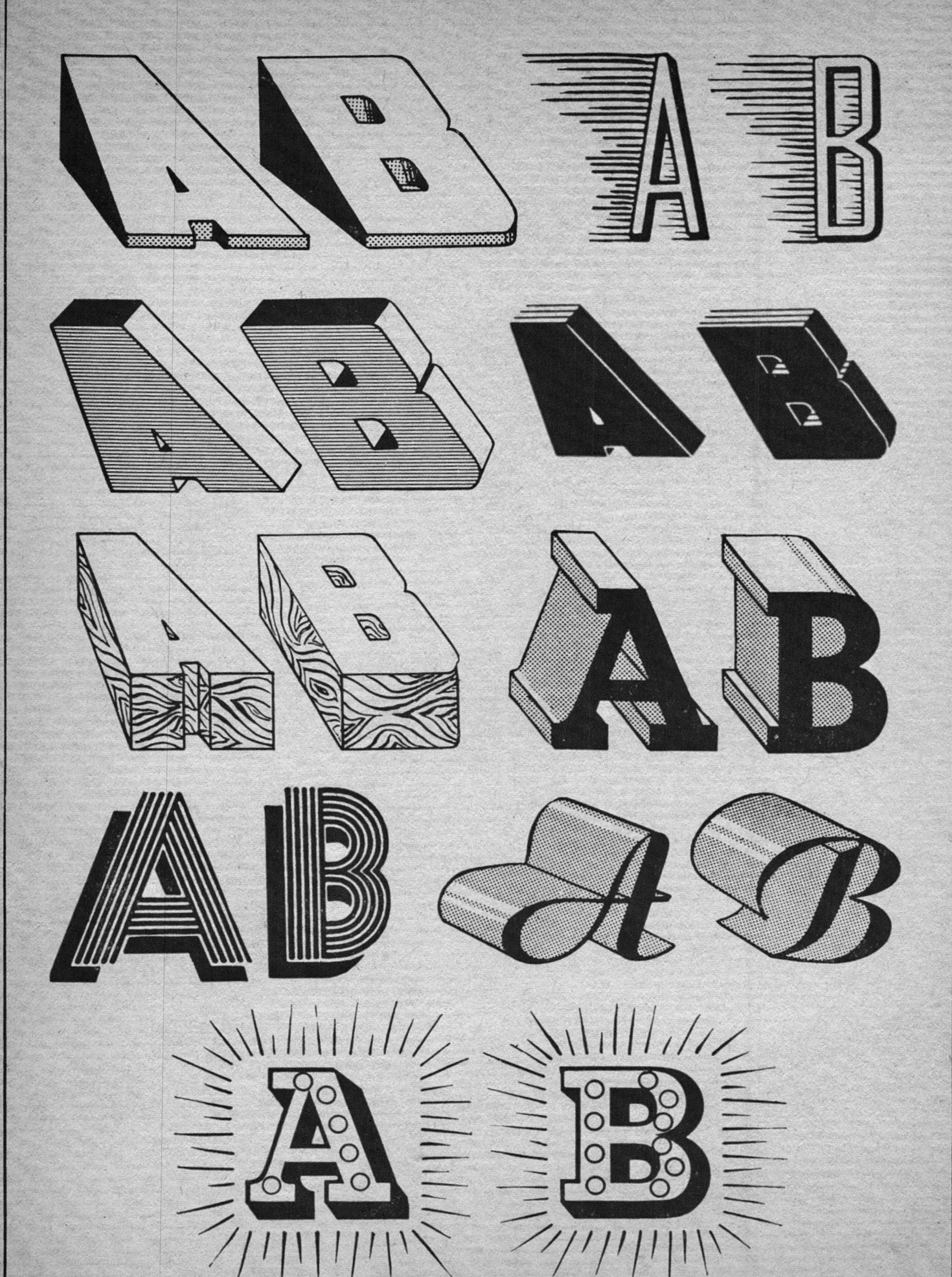

A B C D E

1 2 K L

3 PERS

4 5 O P

S T U V W

F G H I J

M N 6 7

VERE. 8

Q R 9 0

X Y Z &c.

Patriot,
JAMES
Our Nation's

OR
Statesman
ARFIELD
Late Beloved

KINDE
R
FROM

GARDS
Sister Annie.

ABCKL

DEFGHI

abcdefghij

klm 1883 nop

qrstuvwxyz

TUVW

G D E
M N O
U V W

BLOCK & RELIEF SHADE

RELIEF SHADE

OFF SHADE

PERSPECTIVE SHADE

ANGULAR SHADE

BLOCK SHADE

CAST SHADE

SPLIT SHADE

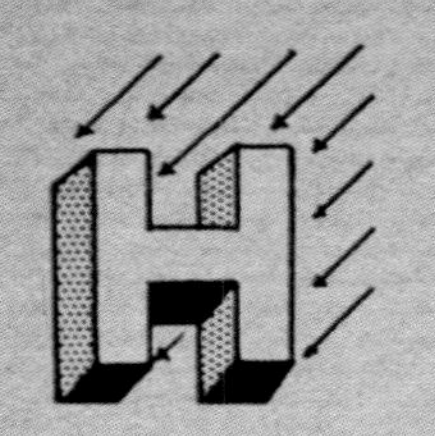

RELIEF

B

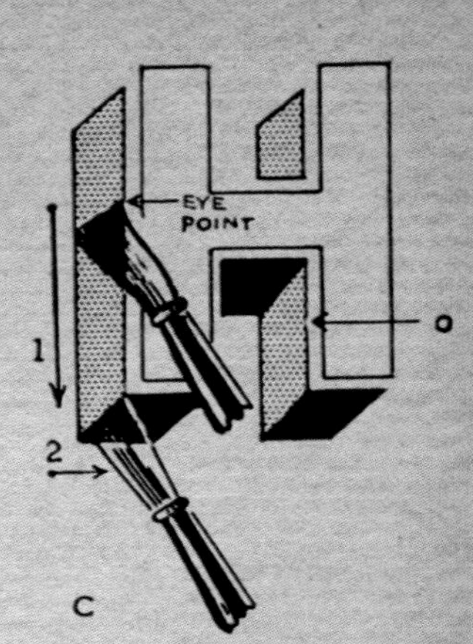

C

CAST SHADE

DROP SHA

CONVEX

F

CON

G 45°

H

I

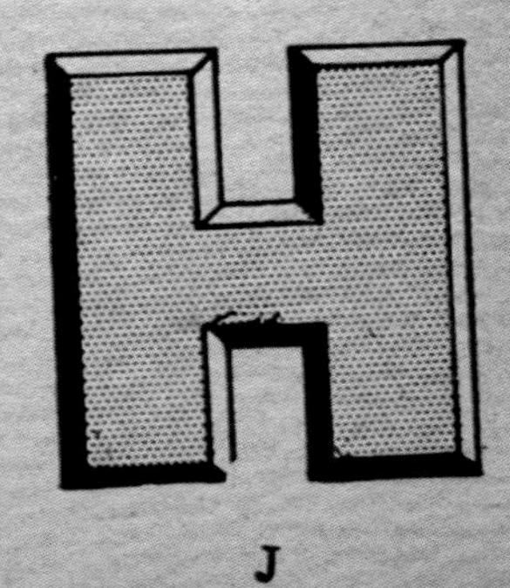

J

ABCDE

FGHIJK

LMNO

PQRST

UVWX

YZ

abcdefg

hijklmn

opqrstu

vwxyz

æœfifl,:.

A B C D E

F G H I J K

L M N O

P Q R S T

U V W X

Y Z

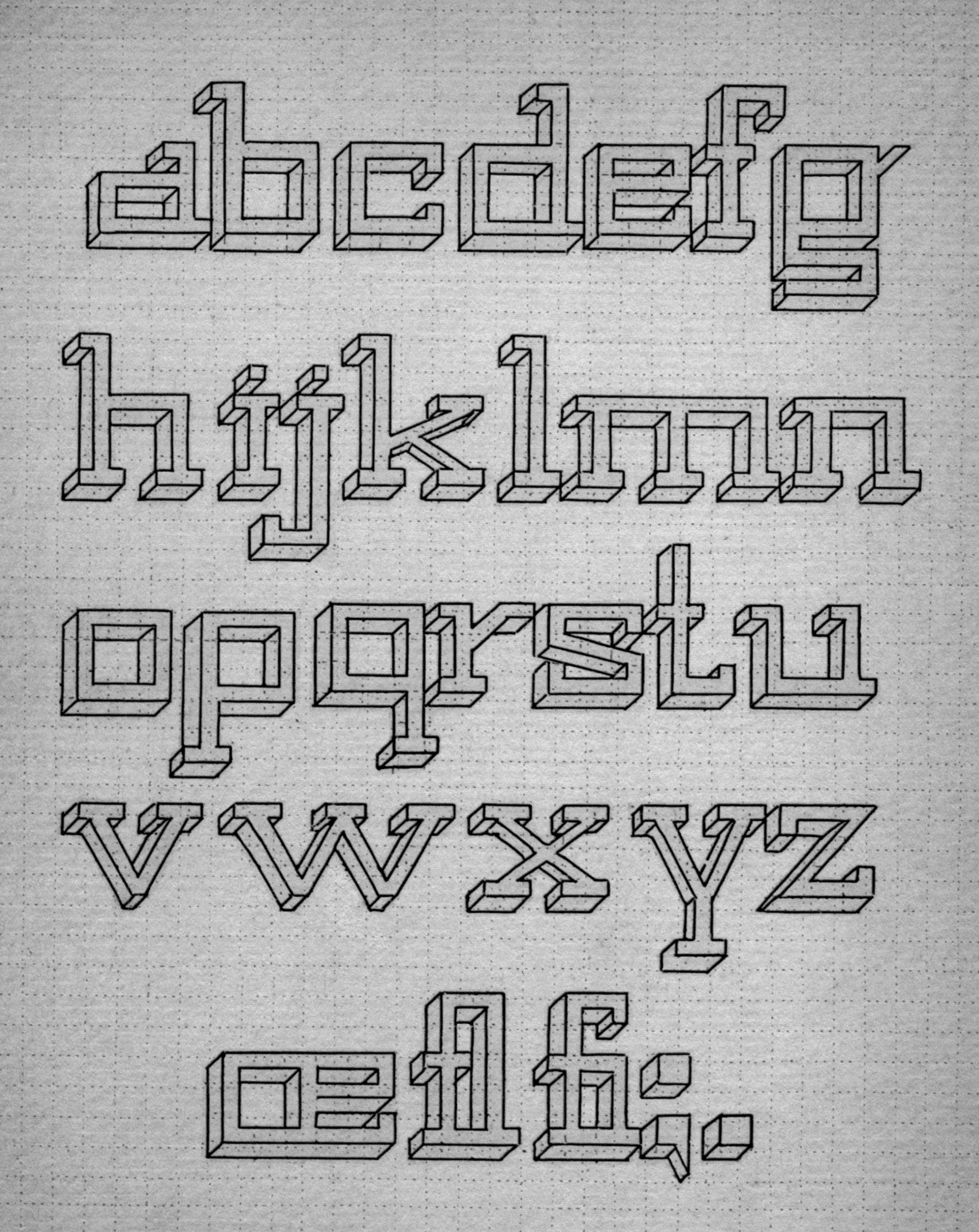
abcdefg
hijklmn
opqrstu
vwxyz

ADSTYLE SHADED

10 POINT $2 50 — 15A $1 15 30a $1 35

TAKING OUR SUBJECT FROM THE STANDPOINT of an artistic printer who selects his ideas from the many surrounding elements that caused the buyers to place their advertisements in his care, we want you to select first a type fitting the 6 work classes

12 POINT $2 75 — 12A $1 30 24a $1 45

SPEAKING ABOUT THE BEST GRADES of typography will never push you ahead in the minds of advertisers and printers who produce 14 results from their effort

18 POINT $3 25 — 7A $1 60 13a $1 65

NO JOB IN A MAIL SACK WILL BOOST ALONG YOUR business advertising if the job is not printorially proper

24 POINT $3 50 — 5A $1 90 8a $1 60

PLACE AN ORDER for nine faces of Adstyle

36 POINT $5 15 — 3A $2 90 5a $2 25

Modern artists SUGGESTION

48 POINT $7 95 — 3A $4 85 4a $3 10

PRINTING color work

60 POINT $11 45 — 3A $6 90 4a $4 55

Expressive BOND

72 POINT $10 50 — 3A $6 40 4a $4 10

SPEAKS stock

This letter expresses Refinement and will make your printed message well received in an atmosphere of Culture

FOR BORDERS, BRASS RULE AND EZEFIT CORNERS, SEE PAGES 18 AND 24

72 Point 3 A 4 a

Great MIND

60 Point 3 A 4 a

PUREST Metal

48 Point 3 A 4 a

Refined BANKER

36 Point 3 A 5 a

INTERESTING HOUSES
Great Demands Created

24 Point 5 A 8 a

CHOICE EXHIBITS
Compounded Metal

12 Point 12 A 24 a

PROCURE IDEAL SPECIMEN
Creating Great Improvement
With Shaded Made Beautiful

18 Point 7 A 13 a

EXPRESSING CULTURE
Conveyer of Refinement

10 Point 15 A 30 a

EXPRESSES REFINEMENT MAKING
It Most Essential in Any Modern Plant
Best Buy on the Market 1234567890

This letter expresses Refinement and
will make your printed message well
received in an atmosphere of Culture

18 Point Shaded Rule 6141
6 Point Tint Dot Rule 5896

VINC
VINC

VINC-A-CAL

KOHLER'S

HAND MADE

BIG VALUE

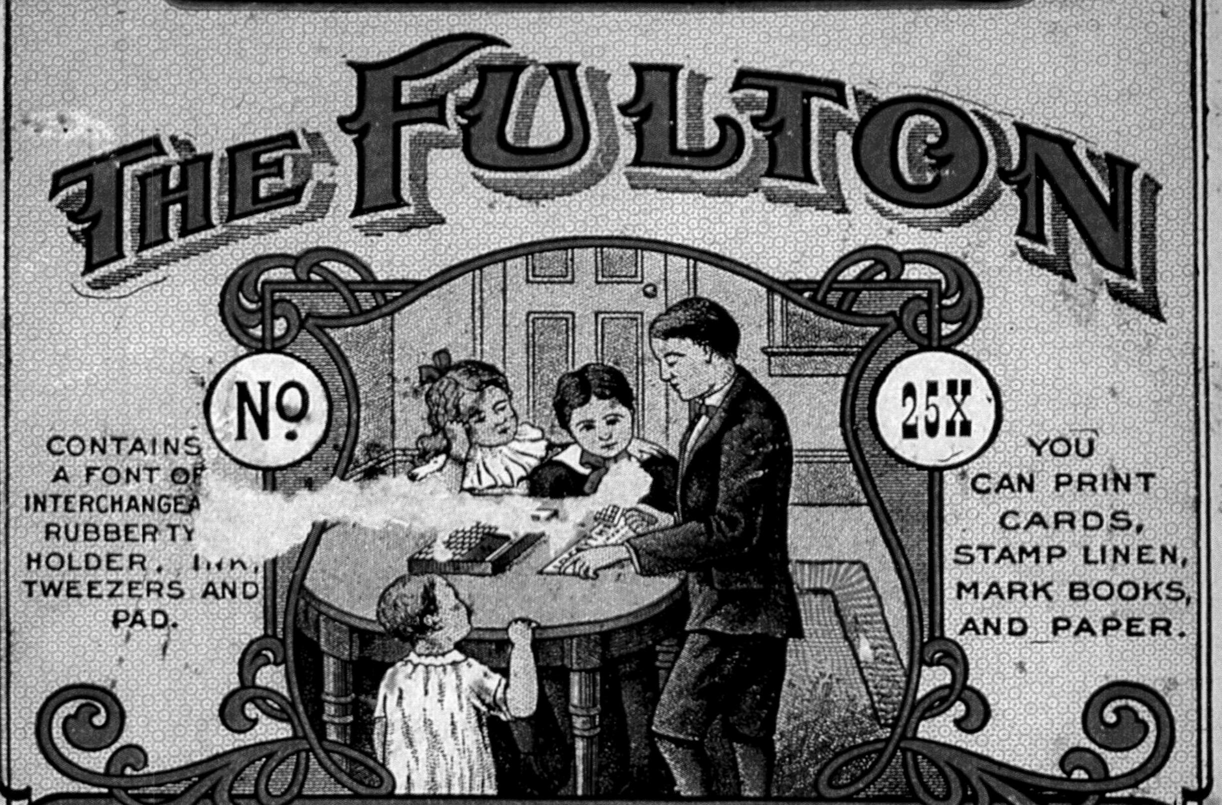

PRINTING OUTFIT

CHEAP. USEFUL. FASCINATING. INSTRUCTIVE

AAAAABBBBBCCCCCDDDDDEEEEEFFF
FFGGGGGHHHHHIIIIIJJJJJKKKKKLLL
LLMMMMMNNNNNNOOOOOPPPPPQQQ
QQRRRRRSSSSSTTTTTUUUUUVVVWWW
WXXXXXYYYYZZZ&&AND 1112222333344455
566677788889999000$$£/d?!.....,,,,,"-⚜⚜

SET THE TYPE OR WORDS AS YOU WOULD WRITE THEM, BUT FROM RIGHT TO LEFT. INK STAMP LIGHTLY ON PAD, THEN PRESS EVENLY AND FIRMLY UPON ARTICLE TO BE STAMPED.

Made by Fulton Rubber Type Co., Elizabeth N. J. U. S.

MILLIONS *sold fo*

THE SAME CIGA

Now
2 for
5¢

EA
EET

5¢ each NOW 2 for 5¢
R

Big

Five
F

THE NEW ART
OF
Modern Cooking

ART MASTERPIECES OF THE

1934

WORLD'S FAIR EXHIBITION AT THE ART INSTITUTE OF CHICAGO

C · J · BULLIET

REPRINTED FROM THE CHICAGO DAILY NEWS
STERLING NORTH OF CHICAGO

B C D E

N O P Q

Z 1 2 3

B C D E

M N O P

Y Z 1 2

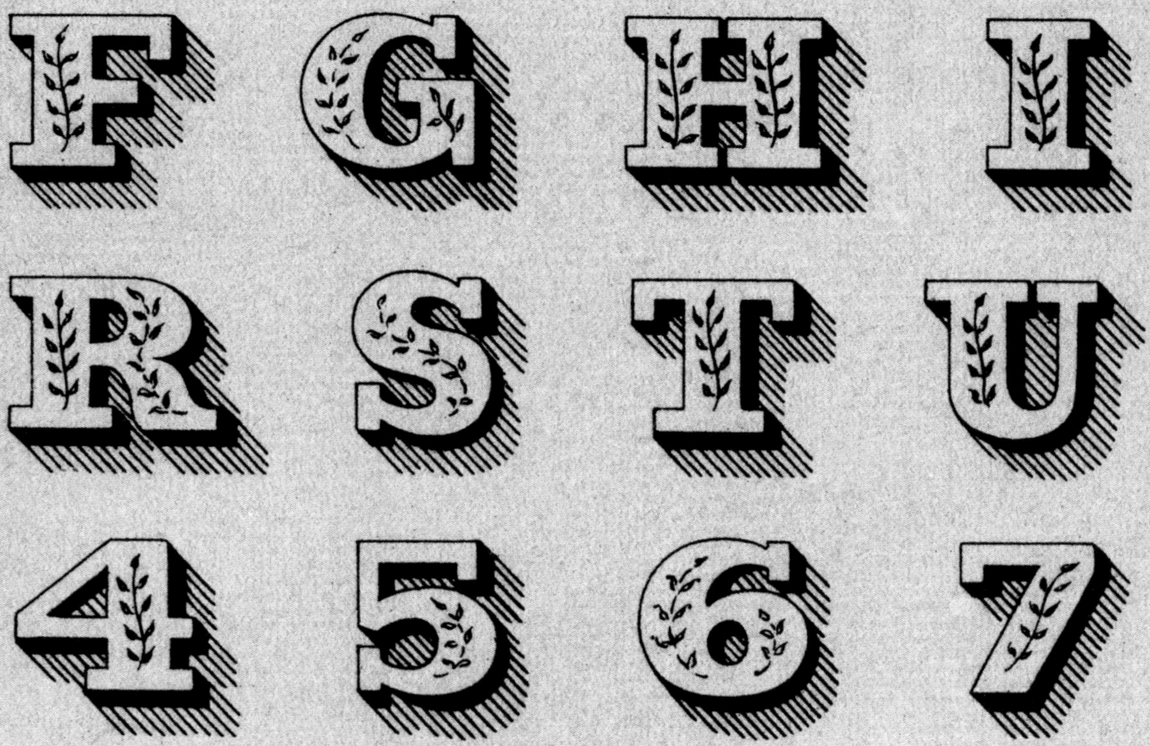
F G H I
R S T U
4 5 6 7

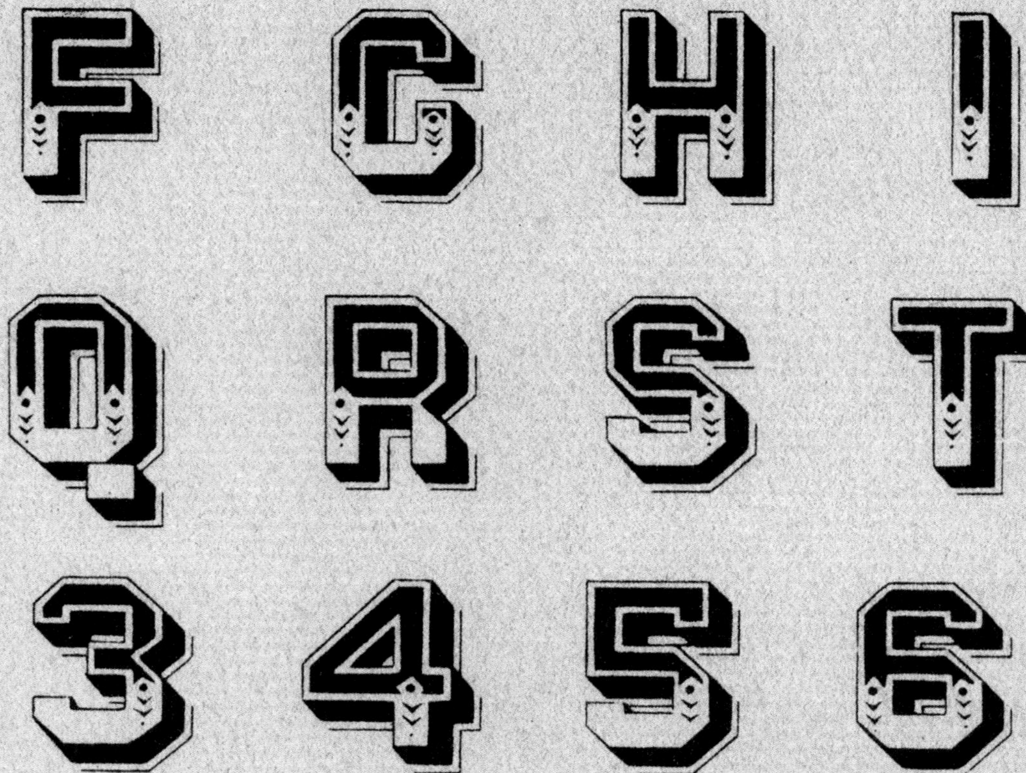
F G H I
Q R S T
3 4 5 6

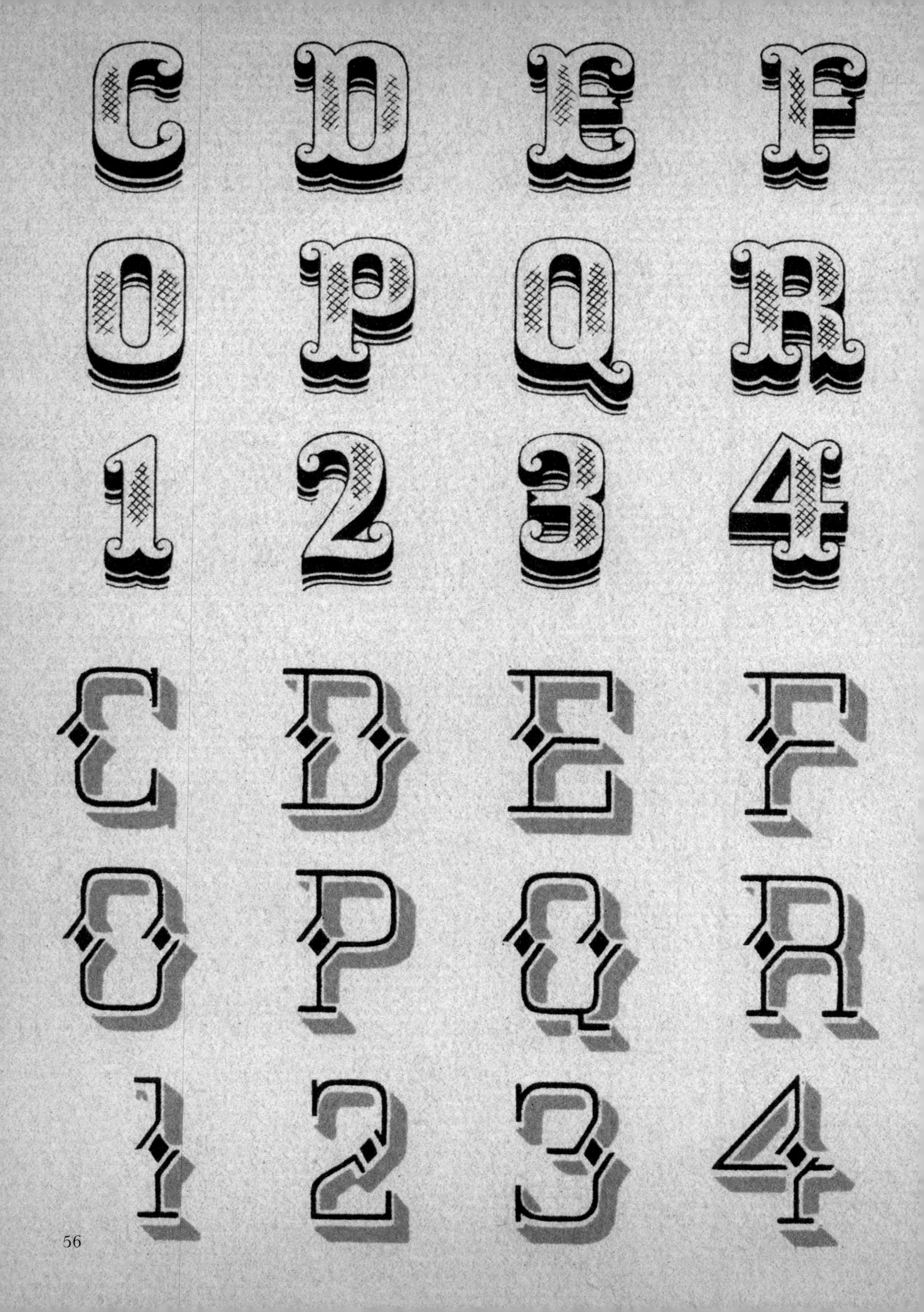
C D E F
O P Q R
1 2 3 4
C D E F
O P Q R
1 2 3 4

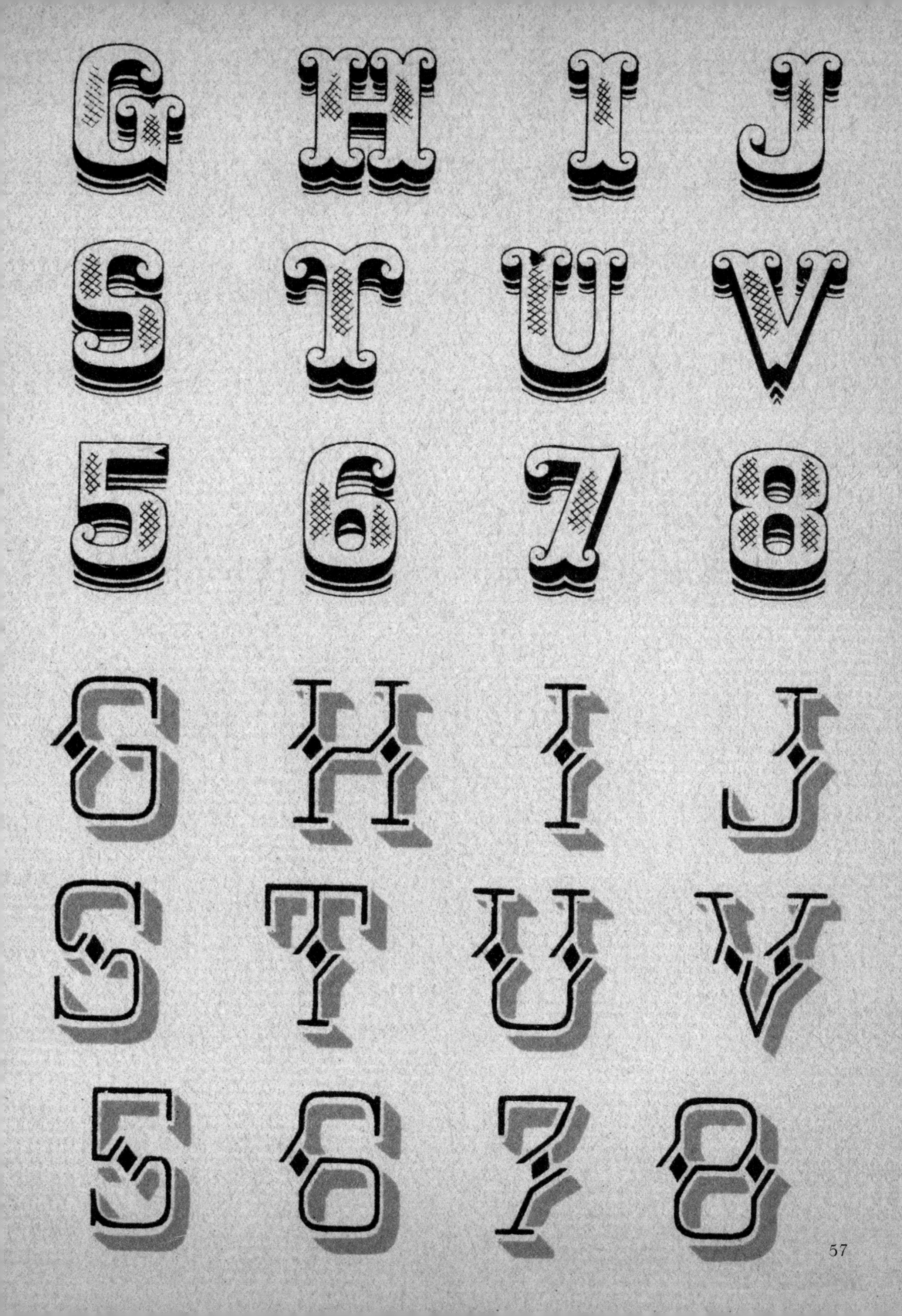

JKLMNOPQRSTUVWXYZ1234567890

EGISTER AND PERFECT IMPRESSION

RIOR TYPOGRAPHIC PRINTING

NN'S EXPRESSIVE PAPERS

TANT ARRANGEMENT

MOBIL INDUSTRY

ISH MAGAZINE

ABCDEFGHIJKL

RSTUVWXYZ1234

ORIENTAL ARCHIT

EUROPEAN SPE

BRITISH PR

EXPLANA

MACHI

CURL

BETON · OPEN

20 Point 15 A

CAMBRIDGE

24 Point 11 A

MONOLITH

30 Point 8 A

PRINTER

36 Point 6 A

TRIBES

48 Point 4 A

COMPETING

60 Point 3 A

MINISTER

72 Point 3 A

ENDURE

84 Point 3 A

FRONT

DEFGHIJKLMNOPQRSTUVWXYZ&$1234567890¢

AGENCY GOTH

OPEN

AN AMERI
TYPE CREA

FOR ATTRACTIVE SET-U

PRINT designed to influenc
is "somewhat like love—one does not *j*
it, one submits to it." And then Cassar
esthetic Parisian, goes on to say that ad
tising "is not a game, but a natural
nomenon like night and day—one of
most beautiful results of contemporar

A B C D
T U V W

REGINA

a Royal Type Face in Capitals

Expressive clarity, achieved by careful hand cutting, characterizes this valuable type face in capital letters.
Alternating black and white, in vivid change of design, determine its graphic value. Of special charm are the efficacious use of hairline and shading.

IN BOO

REGI

ACH

SPE

THE SHADED TYPE

24 point small no. 301020a 9×A 9×1

FROM BERTHOLD

24 point large no. 301024a 8×A 8×1

F G H I J K L M N O P Q R S

Y Z 1 2 3 4 5 6 7 8 9 0 $

TITLES AND ADVERTISING

30 point no. 301028 a 7×A 7×1

A WILL STAND OUT. IT

36 point no. 301036 a 6×A 6×1

EVES IMPRESSIVE

48 point no. 301048 a 5×A 4×1

CIAL RESULTS

60 point no. 301060 a 3×A 3×1

ADVERTISING DISPLAYS

Reg. U S Pat. Off.

VOLUME ONE — NUMBER SEVEN SEPTEMBER 1937

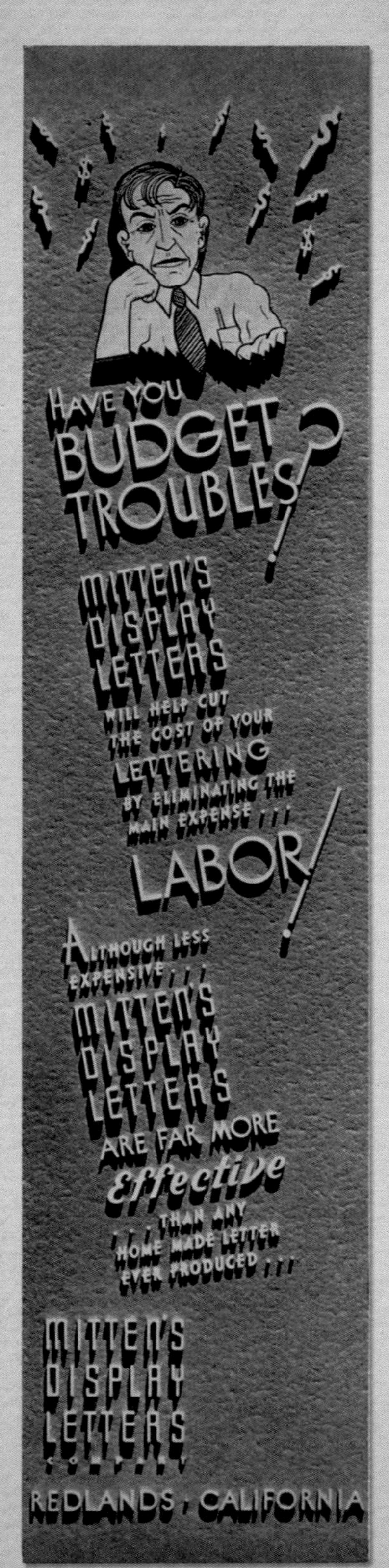
HAVE YOU
BUDGET
TROUBLES?
MITTEN'S
DISPLAY
LETTERS
WILL HELP CUT
THE COST OF YOUR
LETTERING
BY ELIMINATING THE
MAIN EXPENSE . . .
LABOR!
ALTHOUGH LESS
EXPENSIVE . . .
MITTEN'S
DISPLAY
LETTERS
ARE FAR MORE
Effective
. . . THAN ANY
HOME MADE LETTER
EVER PRODUCED . . .
MITTEN'S
DISPLAY
LETTERS
COMPANY
REDLANDS, CALIFORNIA

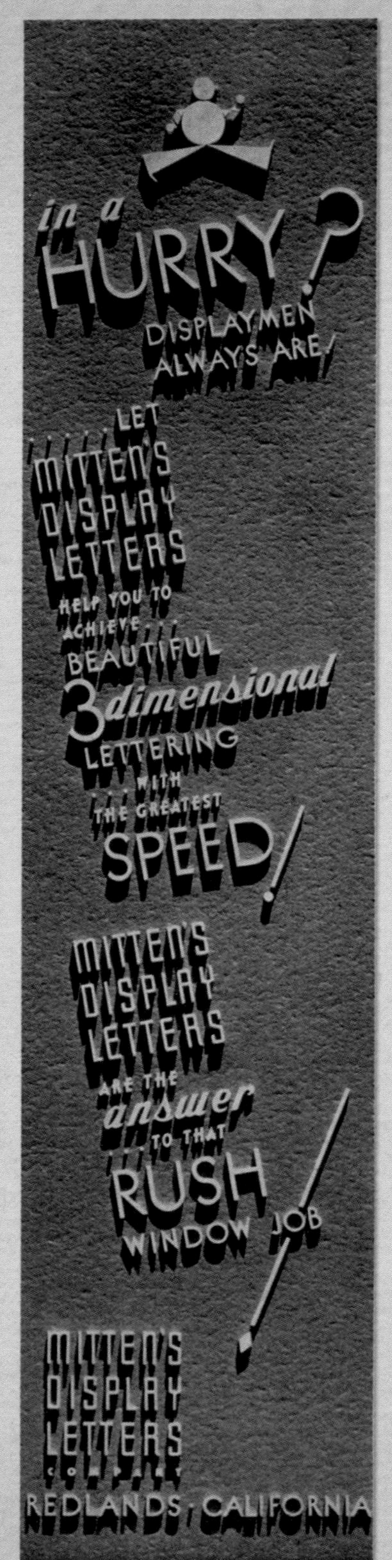
in a
HURRY?
DISPLAYMEN
ALWAYS ARE!
. . . LET
MITTEN'S
DISPLAY
LETTERS
HELP YOU TO
ACHIEVE . . .
BEAUTIFUL
3 dimensional
LETTERING
. . . WITH
THE GREATEST
SPEED!
MITTEN'S
DISPLAY
LETTERS
ARE THE
answer
. . . TO THAT
RUSH
WINDOW JOB
MITTEN'S
DISPLAY
LETTERS
COMPANY
REDLANDS, CALIFORNIA

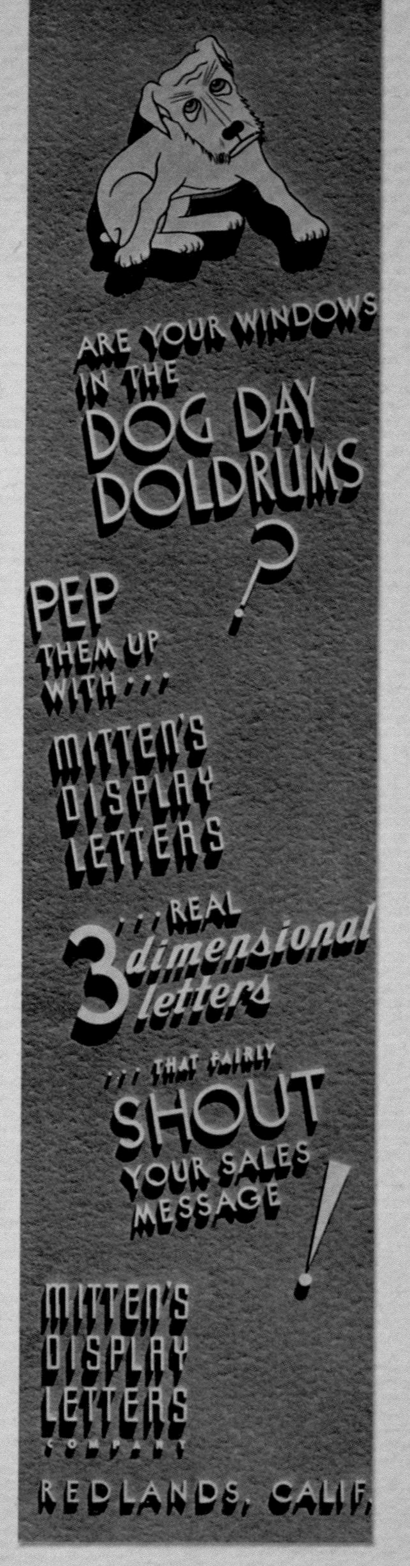
ARE YOUR WINDOWS
IN THE
DOG DAY
DOLDRUMS
?
PEP
THEM UP
WITH . . .
MITTEN'S
DISPLAY
LETTERS
. . . REAL
3 dimensional
letters
. . . THAT FAIRLY
SHOUT
YOUR SALES
MESSAGE
!
MITTEN'S
DISPLAY
LETTERS
COMPANY
REDLANDS, CALIF.

Sho Cards
SIGNS
BROWN SIGN CO.
We Specialize in
Designing
Store Fronts
Displays
Backgrounds
Processing
Pictorial
TRUCK & WINDOW LETTERING
Brown Sign Co.

WALTER'S FLOWERS
BONDED MEMBER
FTD
Telephone
Telegraph

FOR YEARS
THE LEADING
JEWELERS
ROUDA
JEWELERS

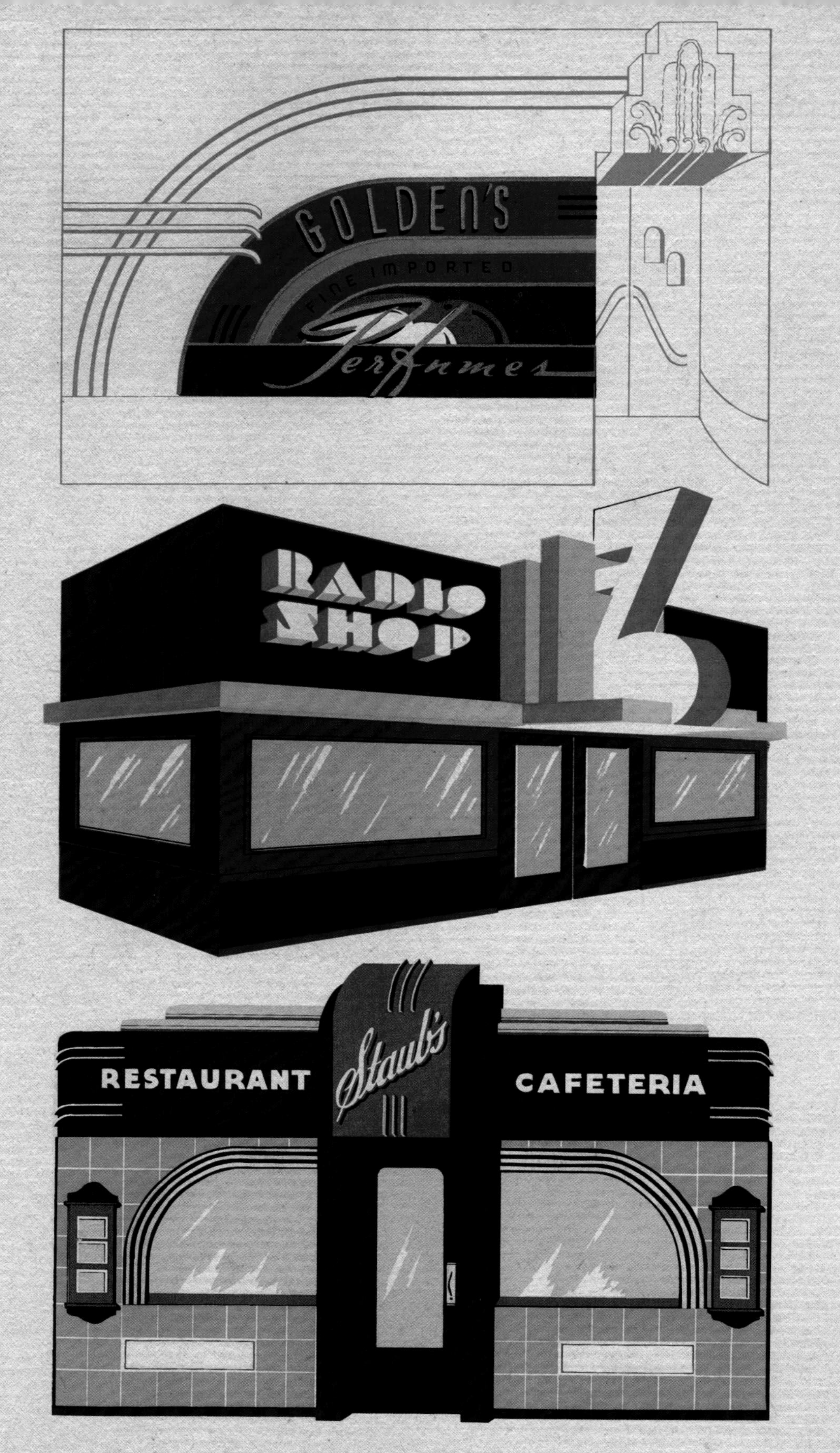
GOLDEN'S
FINE IMPORTED
Perfumes
RADIO
SHOP
Staub's
RESTAURANT
CAFETERIA

NO. 4 IN A SERIES

PACKAGING CASE HISTORIES

... FROM THE FILES OF

BLUES BY

BASIE

LENO

101

columbia record

SING

HOUSEHOLD CLEANER

REMOVES DIRT EASILY
FOR DISHES • WOODWORK
AND GENERAL HOUSEHOLD
CLEANING

KIND
TO YOUR
HANDS

The BEST SELLER

THE ELF
PUBLISHERS
NEW YORK
$2.50

AT YOUR

NEVER CAKES OR
MORTON'S
IODIZED
SALT
IT POURS
MORTON SALT COMPANY
ACCEPTED
AMERICAN
MEDICAL
ASSN.
Committee
on Foods

GROCER

BABY'S FIRST
BOOK

DILLINGER

Copyright MCMXLV
By MONOGRAM PICTURES CORPORATION

Featuring
EDMUND LOWE
ANNE JEFFREYS

IN
"LIBELED LADY"
WITH
WALTER CONNOLLY

COPYRIGHT MCMXXXVI IN U.S.A.
BY METRO-GOLDWYN-MAYER CORPORATION
ALL RIGHTS IN THIS MOTION PICTURE
RESERVED UNDER INTERNATIONAL CONVENTIONS
PASSED BY THE NATIONAL BOARD OF REVIEW

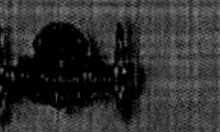

CONTROLLED
BY
LOEW'S INCORPORATED

Directed by
Jack Conway

THE
FOUNTAINHEAD

GARY
COOPER
PATRICIA
NEAL
IN

·42nd STREET·

DIRECTED BY
LLOYD BACON

DANCES & ENSEMBLES
CREATED & STAGED BY
BUSBY BERKELEY

WORDS & MUSIC BY
AL DUBIN and HARRY WARREN

In
Howard Hawks' Production
of
BRINGING UP BABY

RKO Radio Pictures, Inc.
Presents
Katharine HEPBURN
Cary GRANT

COPYRIGHT MCMXXXVIII · · · RKO RADIO PICTURES, INC.
RECORDED BY RCA VICTOR SYSTEM · ALL RIGHTS RESERVED

THE 39 STEPS

GOLD DIGGERS of 1933

IN
"THEY DRIVE
BY NIGHT"
JACK L. WARNER
IN CHARGE OF PRODUCTION

GEORGE RAFT
ANN SHERIDAN
IDA LUPINO
HUMPHREY BOGART

WITH
GALE PAGE
ALAN HALE
ROSCOE KARNS
JOHN LITEL
GEORGE TOBIAS
A WARNER BROS.-FIRST NATIONAL PICTURE

DIRECTED BY
RAOUL WALSH

HOWARD HUGHES
PRESENTS
SCARFACE
FROM THE BOOK
BY
ARMITAGE TRAIL
COPYRIGHT MCMXXXII BY THE CADDO COMPANY, INC.

IN

"EACH DAWN I DIE"

JACK L. WARNER IN CHARGE OF PRODUCTION

JAMES CAGNEY AND GEORGE RAFT

WITH
JANE BRYAN
GEORGE BANCROFT
MAXIE ROSENBLOOM
STANLEY RIDGES
ALAN BAXTER
VICTOR JORY
A FIRST NATIONAL PICTURE

EXECUTIVE PRODUCER
HAL B. WALLIS

ASSOCIATE PRODUCER
DAVID LEWIS

DIRECTED BY
WILLIAM KEIGHLEY

SCREEN PLAY BY
NORMAN REILLY RAINE
AND WARREN DUFF

FROM THE NOVEL BY
JEROME ODLUM

Make Way For Tomorrow

A LEO McCAREY Production

COPYRIGHT MCMXXXVII by PARAMOUNT PICTURES INC. ALL RIGHTS RESERVED

WITH
VICTOR MOORE
BEULAH BONDI
FAY BAINTER
THOMAS MITCHELL
PORTER HALL
BARBARA READ

COLUMBIA PICTURES CORPORATION
presents
Cary Grant AND Jean Arthur
IN

WITH
Richard Barthelmess
Rita Hayworth
Thomas Mitchell
Allyn Joslyn

"THREE ON A MATCH"

DIRECTED BY
· MERVYN LeROY ·

The End

WB
THE END
A FIRST NATIONAL
PICTURE

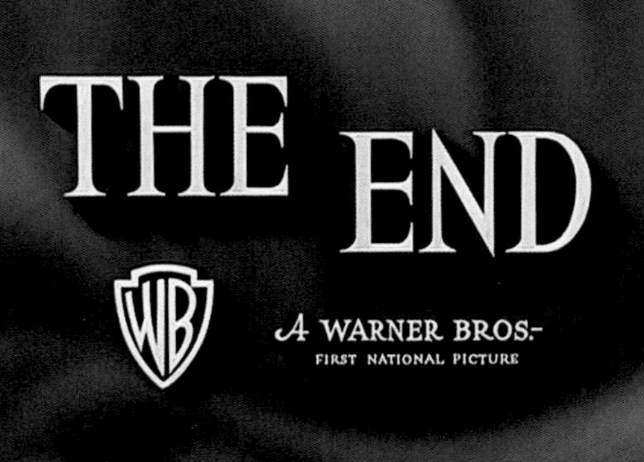
THE END
WB
A WARNER BROS.-
FIRST NATIONAL PICTURE

WARNER BROS. PICTURES, Inc.
& THE VITAPHONE CORP.
WB
The End
COPYRIGHT MCMXXXII · WARNER BROS. PICTURES, Inc.

The End
THE END

SUN
PRINCE
BRAND

FALLBROO

FALLBROO
CITRUS AS
GROWN IN U.S.

RICHLAND
BRAND
PRODUCE
FOUR STAR
BRAND
4
REG. U.S. PAT. OFF.
WASHINGTON
APPLES
PRODUCT OF U.S.A.
CONTENTS ONE BUSHEL

PACKED & SHIPPED BY
F. H. HOGUE CO.
YUMA, ARIZONA
FIREBAUGH, CALIFORNIA

BUX

PRODUCE OF U.S.A.

©STECHER-TRAUNG S. F., CALIF.

BRAND

PRODUCE OF U.S.A.

BONNIE BABE

SHIPPING IN SEASON
FROM
CALIFORNIA and ARIZONA

Lettuce

MAIN OFFICE

PRODUCE OF U. S. A.

Plenti Grand

SELECTED
CALIFORNIA
AND ARIZONA
VEGETABLES
IN SEASON

GROWN, PACKED AND SHIPPED BY
J. (BUD) VUKASOVICH CO.
MAIN OFFICE
WATSONVILLE, CALIF.

AUTHORIZED & COPYRIGHT, 1947
BY JU-C ORANGE OF AMERICA
TRADE MARK

CY

REGISTERED

NGE

fresh

MISSION
ICE

COLD
DAIRY
MISSION
ORANGE
DRINK
FRESH

SEBA
QUA
CALI
AP

TOPOL

LITY®

ity

RNIA

ES

BRAND

PACKED BY

PELLETTI FRUIT CO.

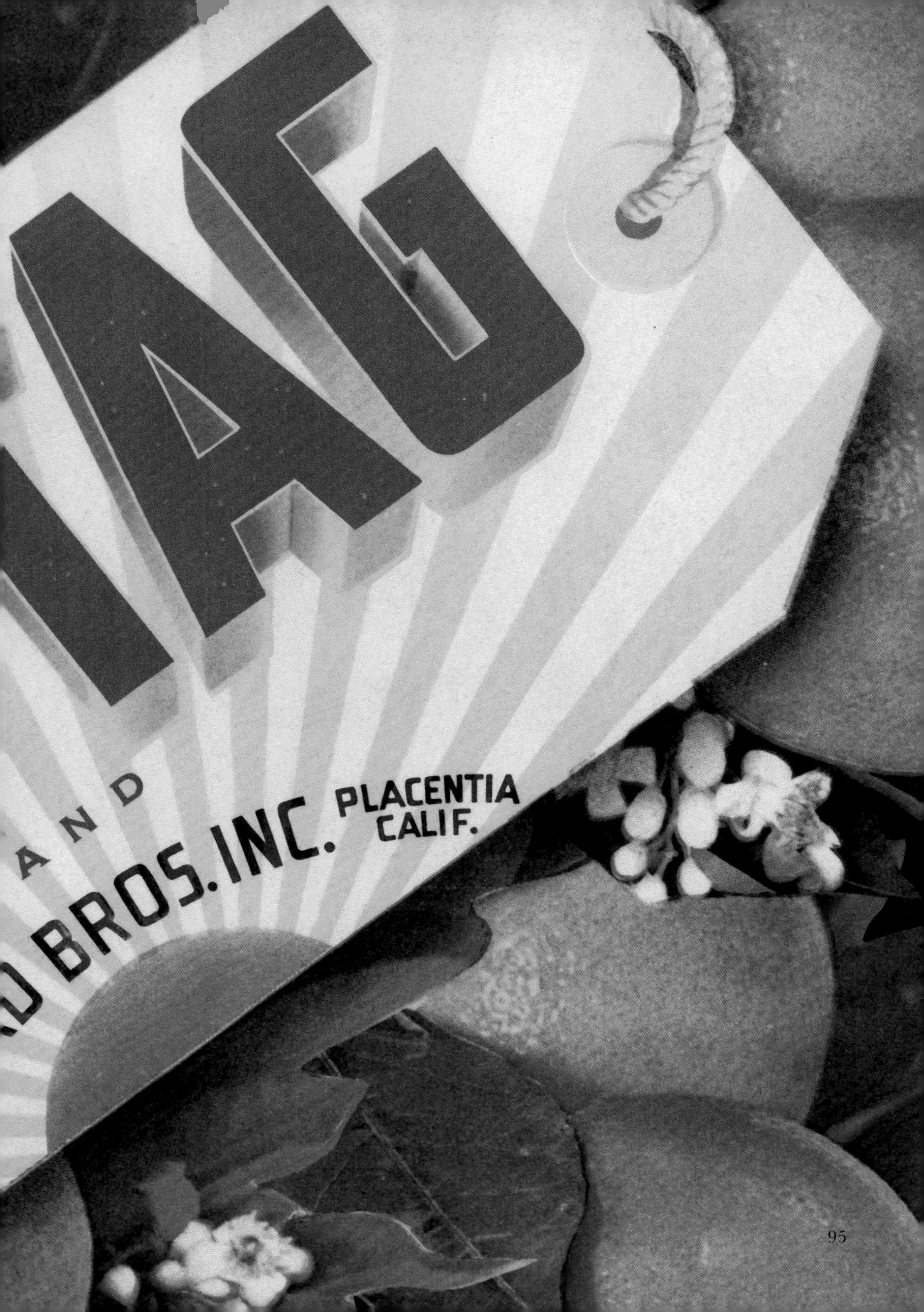

TAG
AND
BROS.INC.
PLACENTIA
CALIF.

JUST

BR

GROWN &
PACKED BY
JAMESON
COMPANY
CORONA
RIVERSIDE CO.,
CALIFORNIA
U.S.A.

RITE

SANTA BARBARA

GROWN A

JOHNSTON

SANTA BARB

GROWN

COUNTY LEMONS

PACKED BY

UIT COMPANY

CALIFORNIA

N U. S. A.

WLS

FAMILY ALBUM

1942

THE PRAIRIE FARMER STATION · CHICAGO

WLS
FAMILY
ALBUM
1934

PM

NO. 19

BERN
HARD

PM

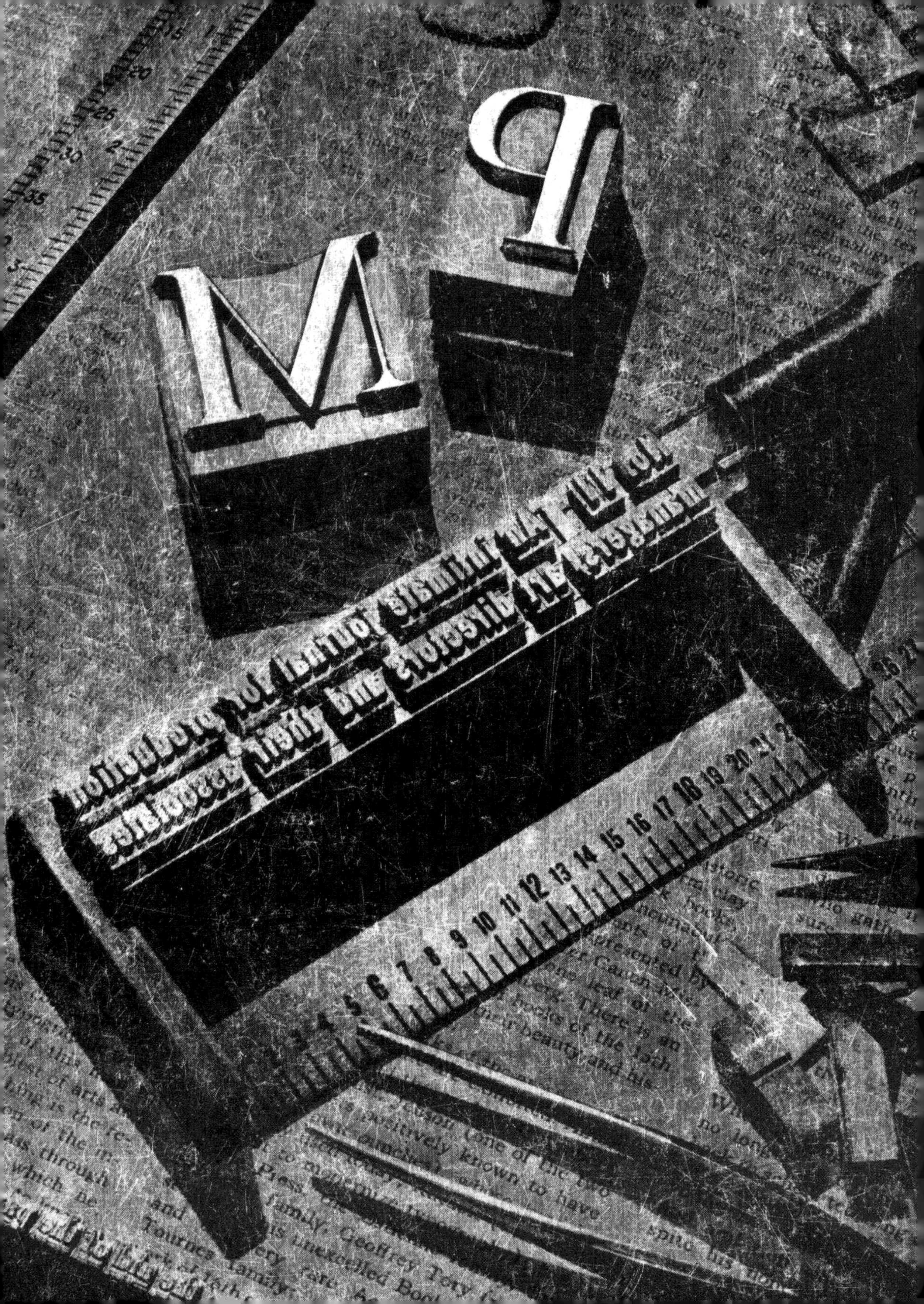

THE AMERICAN PRINTER

for MAY

VOLUME NUMBER NINETY-EIGHT / ISSUE NUMBER FIVE

Price 25 Cents a Copy
$3.00 a Year

ADVERTISING ARTS
A SUPPLEMENT TO
ADVERTISING & SELLING
JANUARY
1931
LEONARD

IMATE
MANAG

THE PRINTING ART QUARTERLY

AND 1936–1937 EXHIBITION OF ADVERTISING PHOTOGRAPHY

Smythe

A DARTNELL PUBLICATION · VOLUME 67 · NUMBER 1 · PRICE $1.50

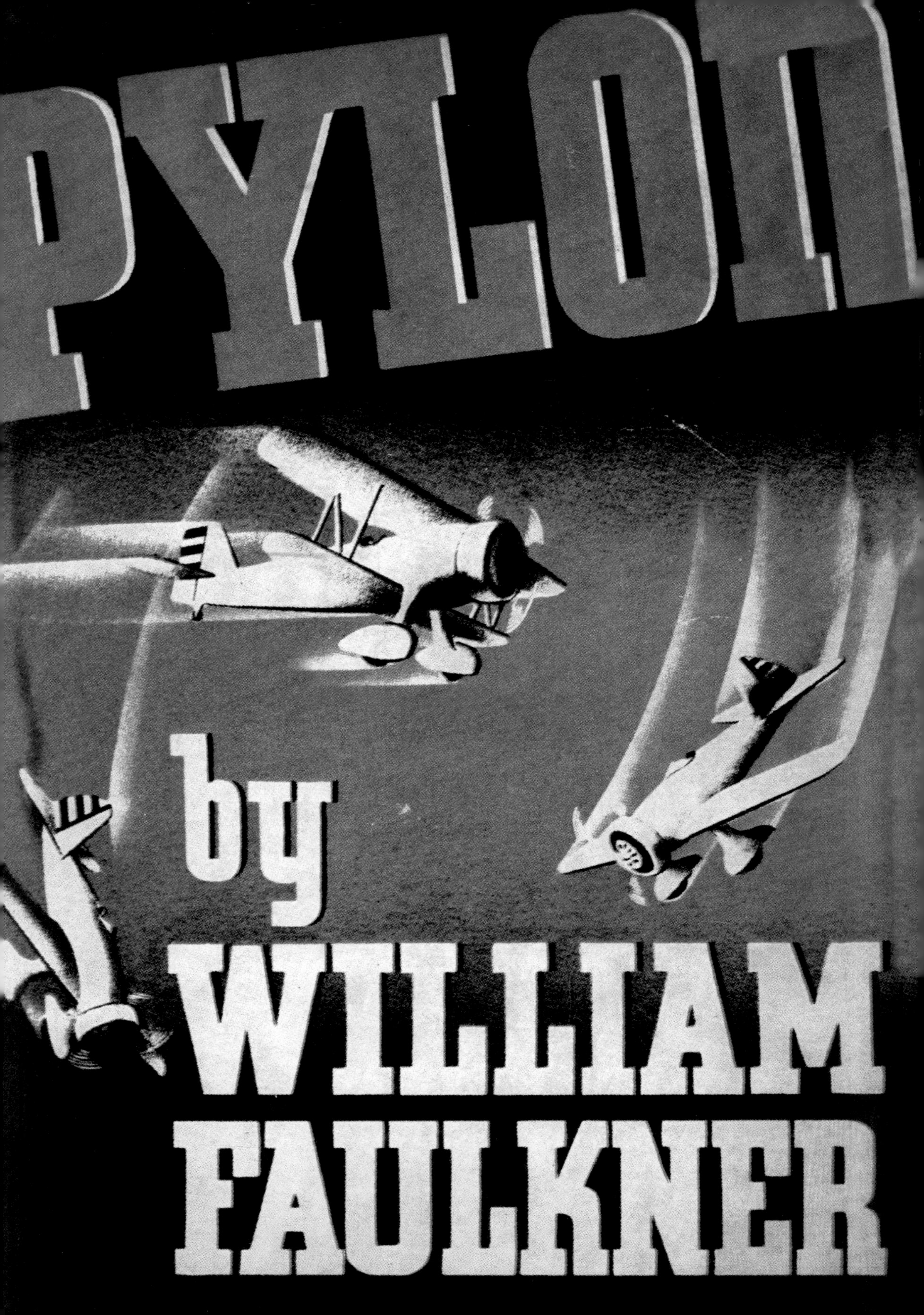
PYLON
by
WILLIAM
FAULKNER

ON THE AIR

M. LEIBOWITZ

RECK
PA
REGISTERED
TRADE MARK.
BL
RECK
PA
REGISTERED
TRADE MARK
BL
CONTAINS
NEW YORK,LO

IT'S
IS
UE
REGISTERED
TRADE MARK
IT'S
IS
UE
REGISTERED
TRADE MARK
DON & HULL.
16 TEN CENT PACKETS
32 FIVE CENT PACKETS

t's New

BLA
783 MADISO
BETWEEN 66TH-

owns

TERNOON EVENING
SPORT WEAR

AVENUE

TH STREETS

GOODYEAR
HIGHWAY OR SKYWAY ...

THERE IS A GOODYEAR DEALER
NEAR YOU

WRIG

MEANS GOOD

WIB

TO

PREFE

MBER

LEY'S

CHEWING GUM

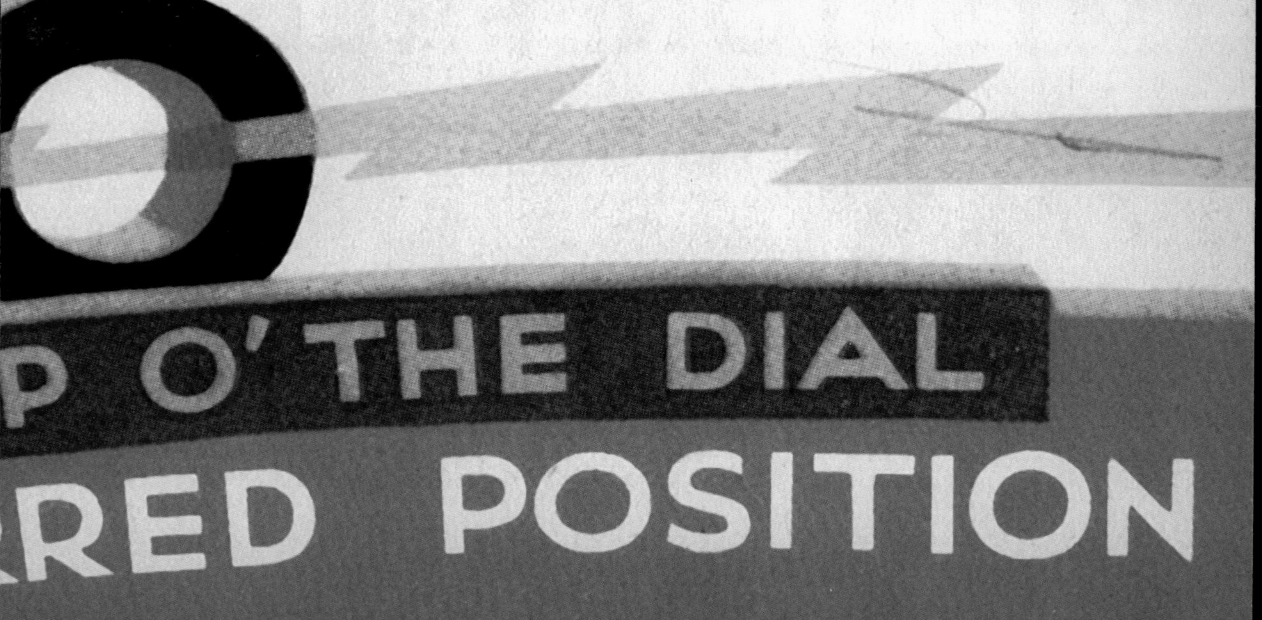

EFFE

EFFE

EFFE

CTIVE

CTIVE

CTIVE

EFFE

EFFE

EFFE

CTIVE

CTIVE

CTIVE

EFFE

EFFE

EFFE

CTIVE

CTIVE

CTIVE

CTIVE

EFFE

EFFE

EFFE

CTIVE

CTIVE

11. Cover of "Burdock Blood Bitters Almanac and Key to Health" brochure, Foster, Milburn & Co., Buffalo, 1892.

12–13. Handbill for the musical *Green Room Fun* performed by Salsbury's Troubadours, New York, 1883.

14–19. Cover and pages from *Palm's Patent Transfer Letters for Wood, Paint, Metal, & C.*, The Palm Letter Co., Cincinnati, 1893.

20–21. Various letter and billheads, *c.* 1895–1900.

22–23. Cover of *Demorest's Illustrated Monthly* magazine, New York, 1874.

24–25. Cover of *Maycock's Educational Drawing Book* by Mark M. Maycock, 1893.

26–27. Specimen pages, *c.* 1920.

28–29. Specimen page of bifurcated Tuscan from *Ames' Alphabets* by Daniel T. Ames, 1884.

30–31. Memorial to former president James A. Garfield set in various shadow styles, 1881.

32–33. Embossed novelty postcard, 1908.

34–35. Engraved specimen pages from *Ames' Alphabets* by Daniel T. Ames, 1884.

36–41. Shadow type glossary and specimens from a correspondence school book, *c.* 1920.

42–43. Specimen pages for Adstyle Shaded from Barnhart Brothers & Spindler's Type Founders, Chicago, 1914.

44–45. Vinc-A-Cal cigar-box label, early 1900s.

46. Kohler's and Artola cigar-box labels, both early 1900s.

47. Package cover for The Fulton Printing Outfit, *c.* 1910.

48–49. "Have a Sweet" embossed cigar-box label, *c.* 1930.

50–51. Big Five cigar-box label, *c.* 1940.

52. Cover of *GE: The New Art of Modern Cooking*, 1937.

53. Catalog cover of *Art Masterpieces of the 1934 World's Fair Exhibition at the Art Institute of Chicago* by C.J. Bullet, designer unknown, 1934.

54–57. Specimen pages from *Letters and Lettering* by Paul Carlyle, Guy Oring, and Herbert S. Richland, 1938.

58–59. Specimen pages from American Type Founders Co., 1940s.

60–61. Specimen pages for Beton Open (left) and Agency Gothic (right) from American Type Founders Co., *c.* 1935.

62–63. Specimen page for Regina from Berthold type foundry, distributed by Amsterdam Continental Types and Graphic Equipment Inc., New York, 1950s.

64. Cover of *Advertising Displays* magazine, 1937.

65. Advertisements in *Advertising Displays* magazine for Mitten's Display Letters, 1938.

66–67. Sample storefront designs from *Original Sign Designs* by the Ohio State Conference of Sign & Pictorial Artists Local Union, 1941.

68. "Packaging Case Histories," advertisement for USP&L, 1937.

69. *Blues By Basie* album cover, designed by Alex Steinweiss, Columbia Records, 1944.

70. Package cover for Sing Household Cleaner, *c.* 1940.

71. Advertisement for *Super City* by Harry Hershfield, 1930.

72–73. Morton's Iodized Salt advertising blotter, 1930s.

74. Advertisement for Calox Tooth Powder, 1920s.

75. Cover of *Baby's First Book*, 1922.

76–77. Film titles for *Dillinger*, 1945; *Libeled Lady*, 1936; *The Fountainhead*, 1949; *42nd Street*, 1933; *Bringing Up Baby*, 1938; *The 39 Steps*, 1935; *The Gold Diggers of 1933*, 1933.

78–79. Film titles for *They Drive By Night*, 1940; *San Quentin*, 1937; *Scarface*, 1932; *Each Dawn I Die*, 1939.

80–81. Film titles for *Make Way for Tomorrow*, 1937; *Only Angels Have Wings*, 1939; *Three On A Match*, 1932.

81. End titles for *Bringing Up Baby*, 1938; *San Quentin*, 1937; *The Fountainhead*, 1949; *Footlight Parade*, 1933; *Libeled Lady*, 1936; *Dillinger*, 1945.

82–83. Fruit-crate labels, 1940s–50s.

84–85. Fruit-crate label for Buxom melons, Firebaugh, *c.* 1940.

86. Fruit-crate label for Bonnie Babe lettuces, *c.* 1950.

87. Fruit-crate label for Plenti Grand vegetables, *c.* 1940.

88–89. Subway-car card for Ju'cy Orange, 1947.

90–91. Tin sign for Mission Orange Drink, *c.* 1940.

92–93. Fruit-crate label for Sebastopol Quality apples, *c.* 1950.

94–95. Fruit-crate label for Sun-Tag oranges, *c.* 1940.

96–97. Fruit-crate label for Justrite oranges, *c.* 1940.

98–99. Fruit-crate label for Harvest lemons, *c.* 1940.

100–101 Covers of *WLS Family Album* radio station magazine, 1942 and 1934.

102. Cover of *PM* magazine, designed by Lucian Bernhard, 1936.

103. Cover of *PM* magazine, designed by Hans Barschel, 1938.

104. Cover of *PM* magazine, designer and date unknown.

105. Cover of *The American Printer* magazine, designer and date unknown.

106. Cover of *Advertising Arts* magazine, illustration by Leonard, 1931.

107. Cover of *PM* magazine, designed by Joseph Sinel, 1936.

108. Cover of *The Printing Art Quarterly* magazine, designed by Smythe, 1937.

109. Cover of *Pylon* by William Faulkner, 1935.

110. Program cover for the Rockefeller Center, *c.* 1940.

111. Cover of *AD* magazine, designed by Mo Leibowitz, date unknown.

112–13. Packaging for Reckitt's Paris Blue laundry whitener, *c.* 1890.

114–15. Masthead for *What's New* magazine, 1930s.

116–17. Subway-car card for Blanat Gowns, 1935.

118–19. Billboard for Goodyear tires, *c.* 1928.

120–21. Billboards for Wrigley's chewing gum and WIBO radio station, both *c.* 1928.

122–29. Specimen pages from *Letters and Lettering* by Paul Carlyle, Guy Oring, and Herbert S. Richland, 1938.

ITALIAN

LIKE SO MANY THINGS TYPOGRAPHIC, DIMENSIONAL LETTERING began in Italy with Roman inscriptions. You don't have to be an epigrapher to see that light shining on letters carved in stone produces subtle dimensional impressions, which evolve as the position of a light source—like the sun, for instance—changes. This ancient history may explain why Italian type designers and typographers have used shadow letters in more contexts than their counterparts in other countries. Nevertheless, in 19th-century Italy, as in the rest of Europe, shadow letters moved into the commercial space, from hand-drawn merchants' signs on glass or wood to metal or wood typefaces. The sign painters' styles and techniques were quickly adapted to print media, largely for functional reasons: whatever was capable of capturing attention at a distance was sure to be even more impressive at close range, particularly in cluttered typographic environments.

Shadows and other multidimensional conceits broke through the forests of unadorned type in magazines and newspapers, but dimension was also used in quieter ways to secure a unique identity through distinct logos, trademarks, or brandnames for products and on packages. Shadows were a customizable device and they could be rendered in a variety of ways. The average Italian printer or designer was not restricted to metal or wood type from a catalog, so many of them created novel type styles with refined dimensional characteristics.

An impression of depth could be achieved in many ways. A close look at the ornate typography on an early 1900s Cav. Salv. Guli & Figli confectionery tin (pp. 136–37) reveals two kinds of shadowing: a heavy gold shadow adds bulk to the company name, making the letters look three-dimensional, while another softer and more naturalistic gray drop shadow—presumably made to look as if it were made by light—raises the words "Confetturieri" and "Palermo" off the surface. Shadows were also used in more modern contexts, however. The Confezioni and Acqua Rapida logos, and the masthead of *abc* magazine (pp. 170–71) are examples of Italian hand lettering from the 1920s and '30s, inspired by both past and present typefaces. Here, the shadows are deliberately more detached and the letters stand in space in a monumental way.

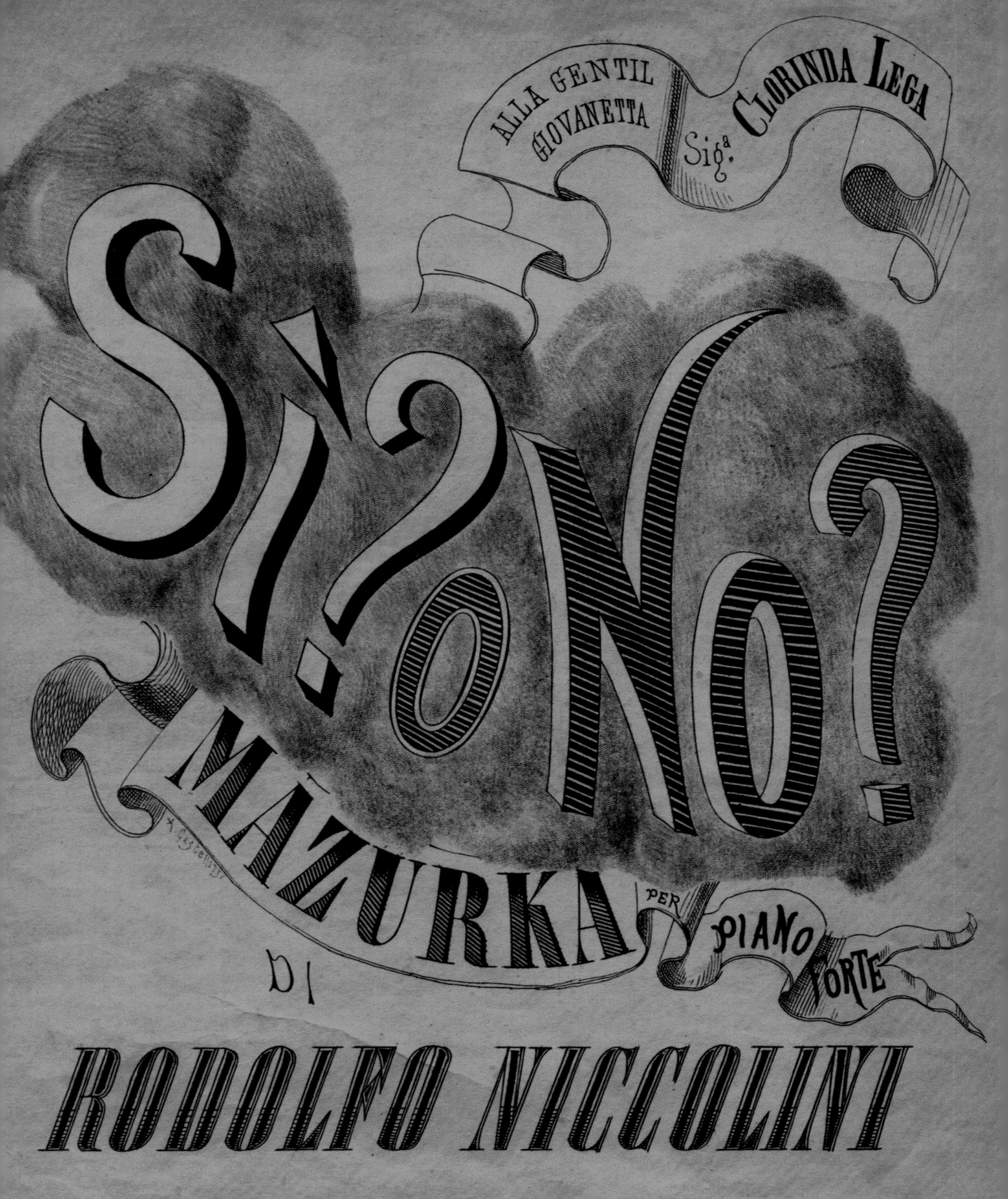

Nº 216 *Prop. dell'Edit.* Fr. 2._

FIRENZE, G. VENTURINI
Via Ghibellina, Nº 100.
Milano, Canti - Venezia, Benzon - Bologna, Trebbi - Livorno, Del Moro - Udine, Berletti

NEGOZIO
in
Chincaglie, Porcellane, Cristalli, Bronzi, ecc.

i, Candelabri
e Lampadari
per Camino
di Fantasia
te a Liquori

GIOVANNI LOREA

Successore

CARLO BERUTTO

PORTICI DI PIAZZA S. CARLO N.º 6.

Ser
da
Me
Alpa

Accad

...rsto

FABBRICA CAMICIE PREMIATA
DI

...DI TORINO

ESP. ITALIANA

C.GI PROCHET, ALBERTI E C.IA

SUC.RI a C. S. CAFFAREL
Piazza S. Carlo, angolo Via Maria Vittoria
Si confezionano Corredi di Lingeria per Uomo e Donna

...A DI GUANTI IN PELLE
...Finti-Colli, Polsini

DEPOSI...
Telerie...

...duto a Mem...

FABBRICA CAMICIE PREMIATA
DI

MED. D'ARGENTO ESP. DI TORINO
1858

ESP. ITALIANA IN ...
1861

M. PROCHET E FIGLI

SUC.RI a C. S. CAFFAREL
Piazza S. Carlo, angolo Via Maria Vittoria
Si confezionano Corredi di Lingeria per Uomo e Donna

FABBRICA DI GUANTI IN PELLE
Cravatte, Finti-Colli, Polsini

DEPOSITO ART...
Telerie Mantile...

Venduto alla Signora Marchesa di Bisio n/di G...
le seguenti pagabili per Contanti senza sconto
Con decorrenza degli interessi per ritardato pagamento
1 Ottobre 1890

TORINO, il

Maison de Chapellerie

VICTOR BESSI

Rome

Rue du Cours 355.

Marquis Bisio Alexandr

...llés ci-après payables à Turin comptant

...FIRENZE

...COU DI MAGLIA

...e, e Fazzoletti

ALLA GIARDINIERA

SAVONELLI & C°

MANIFATTURA D'ABITI PER UOMINI E RAGAZZ

TORINO	VENEZIA	ROMA
Via Po N°. 1	22 Marzo	Via Corso 300

...chese Bisio Gattinara

LAVORI E PROVVISTE FATTE DA

CATTERINA VED. CHIABODO

MATERASSAIA

...ia Lagrange

Casa Colombo

N°-17

CAV. SALV.
CONFETTURIERI
Provveditori delle R.R. Case d'Italia
MECKLENBURG SCHWERIN
E DI PORTOGALLO
PREMIATI
CON 66 MEDAGLIE D'ORO E D'ARGENTO
E DIPLOMI D'ONORE
ALL'ESP. NAZIONALE DEL 1891 IN PALERMO

ULÌ E FIGLI
CAV. AL MERITO DEL LAVORO
PALERMO
NAZIONALE
CASA FONDATA NEL 181

PASTI

BES

VIA CAPPELLARI N.7
MILANO

PROP. ARTISTICA RISERVATA

ANDORO

PANE

BANA

BES

ONE

CERIA

TELEFONO
89-833

F.lli Monteverdi Via Brioschi 33 Milano

BABA'

ONICO

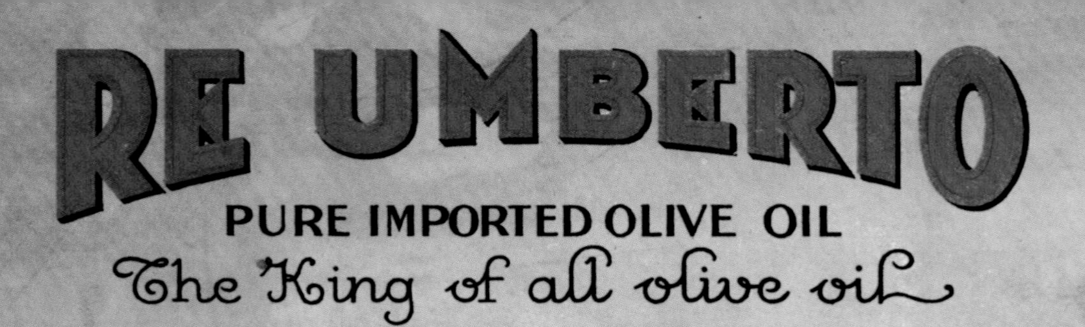
RE UMBERTO
PURE IMPORTED OLIVE OIL
The King of all olive oil

OLIVE
OIL
RE UMBERTO
RE UMBERTO
R.U.
RE UMBERTO BRAND
REG. U.S. PAT. OFF.
PURE
IMPORTED
OLIVE OIL
FOR TABLE AND MEDICINAL PURPOSES
GUARANTY OF PURITY
NET 2 FLUID OUNCES
STROHMEYER & ARPE CO. IMPORTERS & PACKERS, N.Y.

LA VITE

e l'arancio

MILAZZO

PRIMO
CENTRO
VITICOLO
D'EUROPA

ITALIANO

MILAZZO

chiarel
G.CONTRATTO

ATO
ATTO
ELLI —
MARCA REGISTRATA
LIT. DOYEN-TORINO

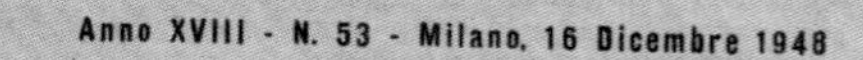
Anno XVIII - N. 53 - Milano, 16 Dicembre 1948

IL CALCIO ILLUSTRATO

30 lire

Abbonamento annuo L. 1350, sem. L. 700
Spedizione in abbon. postale. Gruppo II

Direzione e Amministra[...]
Piazza C. Erba [...]

IN QUESTO NUMERO
un film "CALCIO ILLUSTRATO" SU Torino-Inte[...]

Il Torino s'involva?

Il Torino si è imposto all'Inter per la superiorità della propria consistenza tecnica di squadra, ed i due punti di vantaggio attuali possono essere considerati quattro, disponendo del « ricupero » col Bari. I Campioni anticipano al girone d'andata la fuga degli anni scorsi? E' forse prematuro dirlo, anche perché li attendono tre trasferte nelle ultime quattro giornate. La fotografia mostra le gambe di Maroso e dell'onnipresente Mazzola, che si incrociano come due spade nello sbarrare la strada ad Amadei.

numero unico

La parola Futurismo deve dominare sulla parola Indipendenza

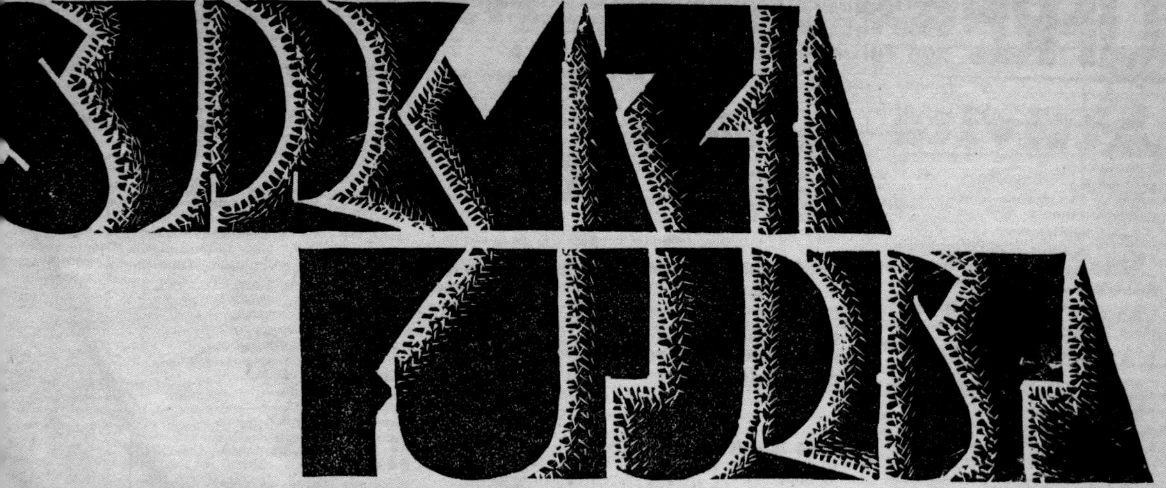

1. [illegible]
Marinetti
2. Combattimento
3. Saluto a F. T.
Marinetti

1

uppi Futuristi indipendenti gui- da Marasco sono ideologica- te in perfetto accordo con il imento Futurista Italiano pur do una loro particolare orga- zione.
futurista, nelle sua tipica as- a libertà può aderire ai Gruppi endenti se li ritiene maggior- e adatti allo sviluppo della pro- attività o non aderire mante- osi strettamente in contatto con ovimento Futurista Italiano di- da F. T. Marinetti.
npossibile però usufruire con- oraneamente delle due orga- zioni.

2

Un venditore di decalcomanie mostrava ad un gruppo di gente cenciosa, in una piazza romana, come era possibile da un semplice pezzetto di carta tirarne fuori tre terribili rivoltelle incrociate, la diabolica piramide numerica di Zoroastro, o la testa somigliantissima di Marinetti, abbellita dai colorini romantici di un tramonto meridionale.
Voila! Tutto fatto con una breve ginnastica del dito indice.
Non originale ma buffissimo quel Cagliostro romano nelle sue arrabbiate dimostrazioni.
La folla sgrana sempre gli occhi dalla meraviglia di fronte alle prestidigitazioni dei ciarlatani, e specialmente i carciofai dei paesi nell'osservare la magica trasposizione delle decalcomanie!
Ma noi, gente smaliziata, ridiamo a crepapelle del fogliolino di carta che assorbe le sembianze di Marinetti, unico ed insostituibile, e siamo i primi a non permettere simili giuochi di carte. Si sappia che i futuristi forniti di buon sangue e di italianissima strafottenza si divertono a scombussolare col loro giocondissimo ingegno l'andazzo funebre dei venditori di decalcomanie. I compagni di Boccioni, di Sant'Elia, di Marinetti e degli squadristi fascisti non possono essere che ragazzi di decisioni veloci e radicali.

E in soffitta la ciarlataneria!
Trenta architetti hanno sorvolato con l'areoplano il fetore di tante discussioni sull'architettura "razionale„ e con orgogliosa risolutezza si arruolano sotto le bandiere del Futurismo. Questi trenta architetti si battono con lo stesso entusiasmo disinteressato e tricolorato col quale si sarebbe battuto Sant'Elia. Non esistono più discussioni sterili o sfumature pessimiste per questi giovani costruttori che sono agilizzati dal vento delle prime clamorose vittorie. Ed è naturale che lo splendore lirico abbagliante - leggerezza vetro acciaio - dei loro "organismi costruttivi„ (vedi nuova Stazione di Firenze: vittoriosa tappa del futurismo indipendente - l'architettura futuristica antibellica Poggi - il piano regolatore delle rombanti città-macchina di C. G. Fiori - i grandiosi aeroporti metallici di Nello Baroni ecc.) procuri le vertigini a chi si ciba di cachéts e a chi ha l'abitudine di vivere nelle case-tomba, negli uffici - polvere scartoffie.... ecc.
Noi "aviatori„ (come direbbe il mio valoroso amico e pilota futurista d'aeroplani Vasco Magrini) sorvoliamo tutte le pozzanghere polemiche e precisiamo subito, per chi ancora non avesse capito, la nostra vibrante passione per il glorioso Futurismo Italiano: religione intensa di Italianità e velocità. Noi, futuristi indipendenti ci sentiamo veramente in perfetto accordo ideologico con l'iniziatore della nuova arte plastica: Umberto Boccioni; col creatore della nuova architettura Antonio Sant'Elia; col Maestro imparagonabile di tutti i Futurismi: F. T. Marinetti.

MARASCO

3

I giovanissimi e i veterani del Futurismo italiano riuniti nei gruppi Futuristi indipendenti guidati da Antonio Marasco, salutano in F. T. Marinetti il capo del dinamismo travolgente, l'ardito di tutti gli ardimenti e il poeta del secolo della Radio e dell'elica trionfante.
I venti anni di Futurismo, di lotte e e di conquiste hanno sommamente contribuito a dare all'Italia il suo volto splendidissimo di Forza.
Lince di forza che si uniscono, si sovrappongono, si allacciano e fanno capo alla passione innovatrice di Marinetti.
La buona battaglia intrapresa per il rinnovamento materiale e spirituale della nostra razza non è ancora finita.
Per noi Futuristi la vittoria più bella è quella che una volta ottenuta ci fa vedere una meta più lontana e più attesa.
Le conquiste ottenute dal Futurismo in tutti i campi sono saltanto oasi sperdute talvolta nel gran deserto della stolta incomprensione in cui ci si riposa per un istante, ci si asseta alla pura fonte dell'orgoglio innovatore e si riprende poi, con più passione, la marcia in avanti.

I Gruppi futuristi indipendenti sono diretti da Antonio Marasco

La Sede Centrale è in Firenze Piazza Signoria 5

DROGHERIA dalla PIOGGI
Fior di salute
Casa del Biscotto
da Ignazio
2749
Valigeria

MERCERIE

ANTICA DITTA
Gppe PELLEGRINI

RISTORI
PREMIATA SALUMERIA
TELESFORO FINI

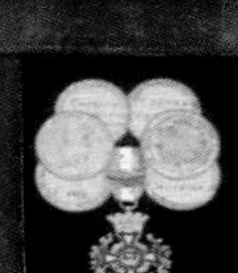

DO FARAI

MARSALA

VINI E OLI

31 R.LE RIANNA

PANTOFOLE

ACCESSORI PER CALZATURE

ALL' ARCO

436

DROGHERIA PRETI

DI ZUIN LUIGI

DROGHERIA

INA
PROPRIETA' ISTITUTO
NAZ. ASSICURAZIONI

Pasticceria

SORARU'
VIRGILIO

BARBIERE

ALIMENTARI
SEBASTIANO TABACCO

A. BONCORDO
1884

DITTA
P. GALLIANI
FONDATA NEL 1819

FORNO A VAPORE
AMEDEO GIUSTI

BECCHERIA

S.re CAMBRIA

ARROTINO

NEGOZIO DI VETTURE
CITTÀ E CAMPAGNA

OROLOGERIA
D. Bacci

OLORI E FERRAMENTA

BONADIO

Lactipan

Il piu' attivo dei
fermenti lattici
STREPTOCOCCUS GUNTHERI
B. ACIDI LACTICI
GLICOBAKTER METSCHNIKOFF
B. BULGARICUS
LACTIPAN

MILANO 20 FEBBRAIO 1929 - VII - c. c. postale - quindicinale illustrato
9
3 lire
SECOLO XX
XX
F. Depero Rovereto
In questo numero:
DIEGO ANGELI
GIUSEPPE BEVIONE
LUIGI CHIARELLI
CRISPOLTO CRISPOLTI
LUCIO D'AMBRA
CARLO LINATI
ADRIANO LUALDI
FILIPPO MEDA
L. A. MONDINI
PIETRO STOPPANI
ERNESTO VERCESI
NICOLA ZINGARELLI
Una musica di
NINO CATTOZZO
QUARANTA PAGINE
DEDICATE ALL'EVENTO
DELLA CONCILIAZIONE

BIENNALE DI VENEZIA

MAGGIO-OTTOBRE 1940-XVIII

RIDUZIONI FERROVIARIE

A/IX° E.F.
ANNO 1° N. 17
12 LUGLIO 1931
GIOVENTÙ FASCISTA

A. IX
ERA FASCISTA
ANNO 1°- N° 26
13 SETTEMBRE
IL FASCISMO NON
VI PROMETTE NÉ
ONORI NÉ CARICHE
NÉ GUADAGNI MA
IL DOVERE E IL
COMBATTIMENTO.
MUSSOLINI
FASCISTA

AMARETTI
DI
SARONNO
LAZZARONI

CROCIERE 1937
D'ESTATE
"ITALIA"
SOCIETA' DI NAVIGAZIONE

AMEBIASI

DIARREE

ENTEROCOLITI

LAMBLIASI

ENTERI

PARASSITOSI INTESTINALI

STOVARSOLO

TAPPEZZIERE

TAPPEZZIERE

CAFFE'
MISCELA
BARBERA
IN
SACCHETTI
DA GR 100 E
200
Barbera
Barbera
Barbera
Barbera
IN VENDITA QUI
autorizzata per tutto il Regno dalla R. Quest. di Milano in data 4 Agosto 1933 - XI. ai sensi dell'Art. 217 Regol. di Pubb. sicurezza.
Grafiche A. MARIANI - Via Mede, 25 - Milano

CARTA
IDEALE
PER
GABINETTO
IGIENICA

DENTIFRICIO

UMBERTO

DENTIFRICIO

UMBERTO

DENTIFRICIO

UMBERTO

DENTIFRICIO

UMBERTO

MATITA
COPIATIVA
Littoria
1 DOZZINA
N. 321
Rosso/Azzurro
VITAMI
METALLI: CA

ADULTI
NIA-VIT
A + B1 + B2 + B6 + C + D2 + PP
MAGNESIO + RAME + MANGANESE + SODIO
TICI - MILANO
EXCELSIOR
HOTEL
ROMA

Art. 625
MARCA
SETA PURA
SETA PER
Esigere

DEPOSITATA
OZZOLO
O REALE
CHIELLI
SETA PURA
12 SPAGNOLETTE

CONFEZIONI

MACELLERIA

ACQUA RAPIDA

SOMMARIO: LUIGI SERVOLINI - *Pittura riminese del trecento:* Giovanni Baronzio — OLGA BERTOLI - Angeli nella pittura italiana — TERESIO ROVERE - Quaderni d'arte — S. L. - *Artisti contemporanei:* G. B. Zaccaria — LUIGI PARADISI - La maschera — GIOVANNI REDUZZI - *Iconografia storica:* Il « Bellerofonte » — FRANCISO VANNINI - *Giovani artisti e giovani disegnatori:* Istruzioni riguardanti lo studio del chiaroscuro — Comunicazioni varie - Avvertenza - Libri.

CASA EDITRICE ABC VIA LUDOVICA, 17-19 - TORINO

stantino Ca

ELECTED GRAPES

rasco Horte

SELECTED APRICOT

MEPHIS
MADE IN CZECHOSLOV
L. & C. HARDT
KOH-I-NOOR
MEP
L. & C. H

ENCIL FACTORY
HISTO
ARDTMUTH

TIVO
RONI
RONNO

DI COLA'S FINEST

ICILY MACARONI
NI DI COLA
ROYAL HIGHNESSES THE DUKES OF AOSTA AND GENOA
HOUSE OF SUPERIOR MACARONI
TRADE MARK
ALL COUNTRIES
UNIVERSAL BARCELONA

C.20. XII
Distribuzione Autorizzata dalla R. Questura di Milano 5 Dicembre 1933.

133. Cover of "Si? o No?" sheet music by Rodolfo Niccolini, late 1890s.

134–35. Various billheads, late 1890s.

136–37. Cover of a Cav. Salv. Guli & Figli confectionery tin, early 1900s.

138–39. Pasticceria wrapping paper, 1930.

140. Point-of-purchase display for Re Umberto olive oil, 1930s.

141. Advertisement for the Milazzo wine region, 1930s.

142–43. Point-of-purchase display for Chinato Contratto, 1932.

144. Cover of *Il Calcio Illustrato* magazine, 1948.

145. Cover of *Supremazia Futurista* newspaper, 1933.

146–51. Hand-painted vintage shop signs in Italy, photographs by Louise Fili.

152. Advertisement for Eparema digestive medicine, *c.* 1930.

153. Advertisement for Lactipan, *c.* 1930.

154. Cover of *Secolo XX*, designed by Fortunato Depero, 1929.

155. Poster for the Venice Biennale, 1940.

156–57. Covers of *Gioventù Fascista* magazine, designed by Mario Sironi, 1931.

158. Poster for Amaretti di Saronno, designed by Marchesi, 1933.

159. Poster advertising summer cruises, designed by Erberto Carboni, 1937.

160. Advertisement for Stovarsolo medicine, *c.* 1932.

161. Logo for Rossi upholstery, *c.* 1930.

162. Poster for Arrigoni, 1930.

163. Poster for Miscela Barbera coffee, 1933.

164. Wrapper for Carta Ideale toilet paper, 1928.

165. Packaging for Umberto toothpaste, 1935.

166–67. Littoria pencil box, Omnia-Vit packaging, and label for Excelsior Hotel, all 1930s.

168–69. Packaging for Seta Bozzolo thread, 1950.

170. Brochure for Gaetano d'Apuzzo pasta and various packaging logos, 1930s.

171. Cover of *abc: Rivista d'arte* magazine,1936.

172–73. Fruit wrapper, *c.* 1947.

174–75. Mephisto pencil box (Italian product made in Czechoslovakia), *c.* 1940.

176–77. Poster for Lazzaroni Saronno biscuits, designed by Marchesi, 1932.

178–79. Advertisement for Giovanni di Cola macaroni, *c.* 1950.

180. Point-of-purchase display for Alana Asso playing cards, 1933.

FRENCH

FRENCH TYPOGRAPHERS DID NOT INVENT DIMENSIONAL LETTERING, but the artistic devices of optical illusionism and forced perspective that were popularized in France during the late Baroque period certainly had a profound impact on the country's subsequent typographic indulgences. The *trompe l'oeil*, a fashionable decorative conceit in the Baroque era, involved painting buildings with false facades, simulating book-filled cases on sitting-room walls and other eye-engaging visual deceptions. By the 19th century, the *trompe-l'oeil* technique had been adopted by typographers—not because it was still in vogue, but because sign painters and printers realized that the volumetric letters both fooled and stimulated people's perceptions. As a result, many early French types were as ornate as the architecture that influenced them. Bifurcated Tuscan types reigned supreme.

Dimensionality was a practical tool for the mid- to late 19th-century French sign painter. Many of the most startling placards and signs—fascia lettering—were actually real three-dimensional letters made from carved wood, molded plaster, or cut metal, attached to or hung from a building or post. They were often visually—if not aesthetically—more impressive than signs painted on glass. In Paris, the city of light, illumination was everywhere, but many French shop-sign makers avoided the temptation to build their words out of incandescent light bulbs. Instead, they illuminated them through indirect lighting. Dimensional lettering could capture the desired effect of radiance. The prowess of the professional letterer meant nothing, however, without an exceptional template as a guide. Consequently, a market arose for portfolios filled with unique dimensional alphabets, often brightly colored and with various shadow options depending on how the sign was to be used.

The jump from the merchant's sign to the printed page was not huge. In this chapter, the shadowing on a catalog cover for Thonet chairs (p. 240) forges a strong business identity. "Real" shadows are photographed and then artfully retouched: the heavy shadows are imposing additions to the capitals spelling out "Thonet," and the majestic effect is magnified by the giant shadows of the two simple chairs that stretch across most of the page, creating a clear impression of monumentality.

CARACTÈRE D'ACTUALITÉ

DESSINÉ PAR MARCEL JACNO

FILM

GRAVÉ ET FONDU PAR

Lilian Harvey
Photo Fox-Film

DEBERNY ET PEIGNOT 18 RUE FERRUS PARIS XIV

F C H
K L M N
P
FLORIDE
S T U
W X Y Z
3 4 5

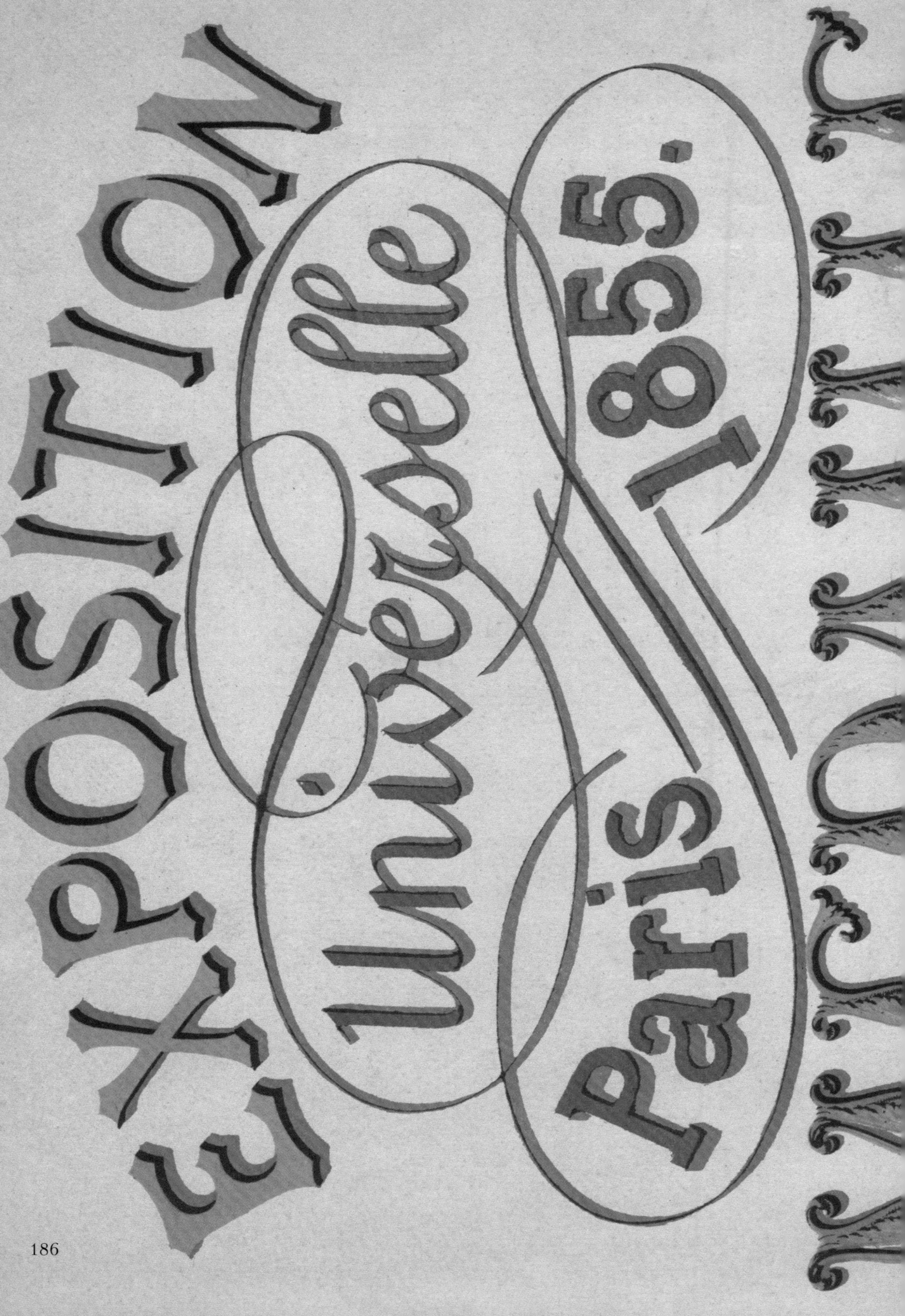

EXPOSITION
Universelle
Paris 1855.

décernée

au Manuel de

PEINTURES

BCD
JKL
STU

EFGH
NOPQ
VXYZ

ABCD

IJKLM

RSTU

EFGH

NOPQ

VXYZ

hijklmn

EFGH

NOPQR

WXYZ.

uvwxyz

LETTRES
L E O N

BRO

ANT

NZE

QUE

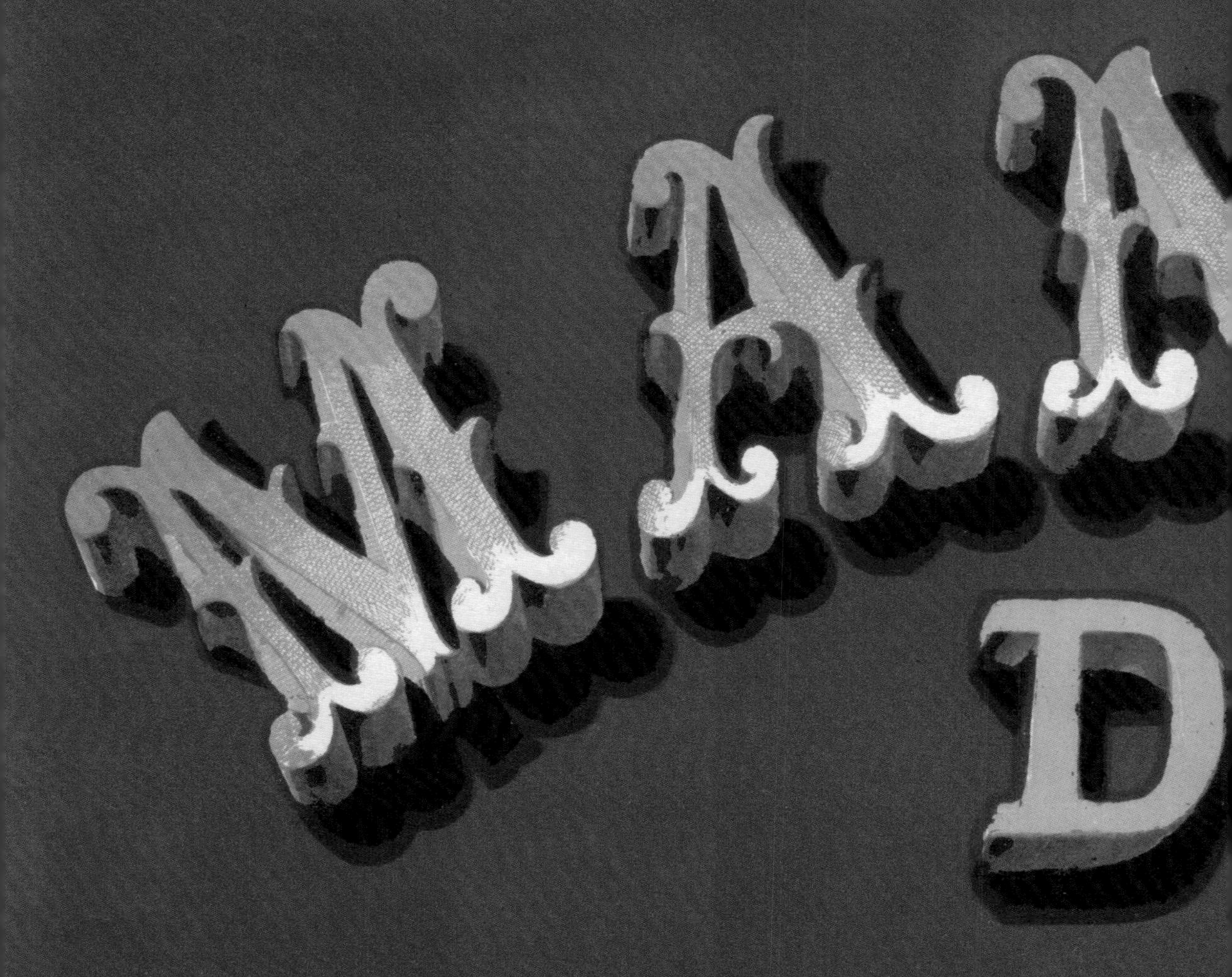

E

URES.

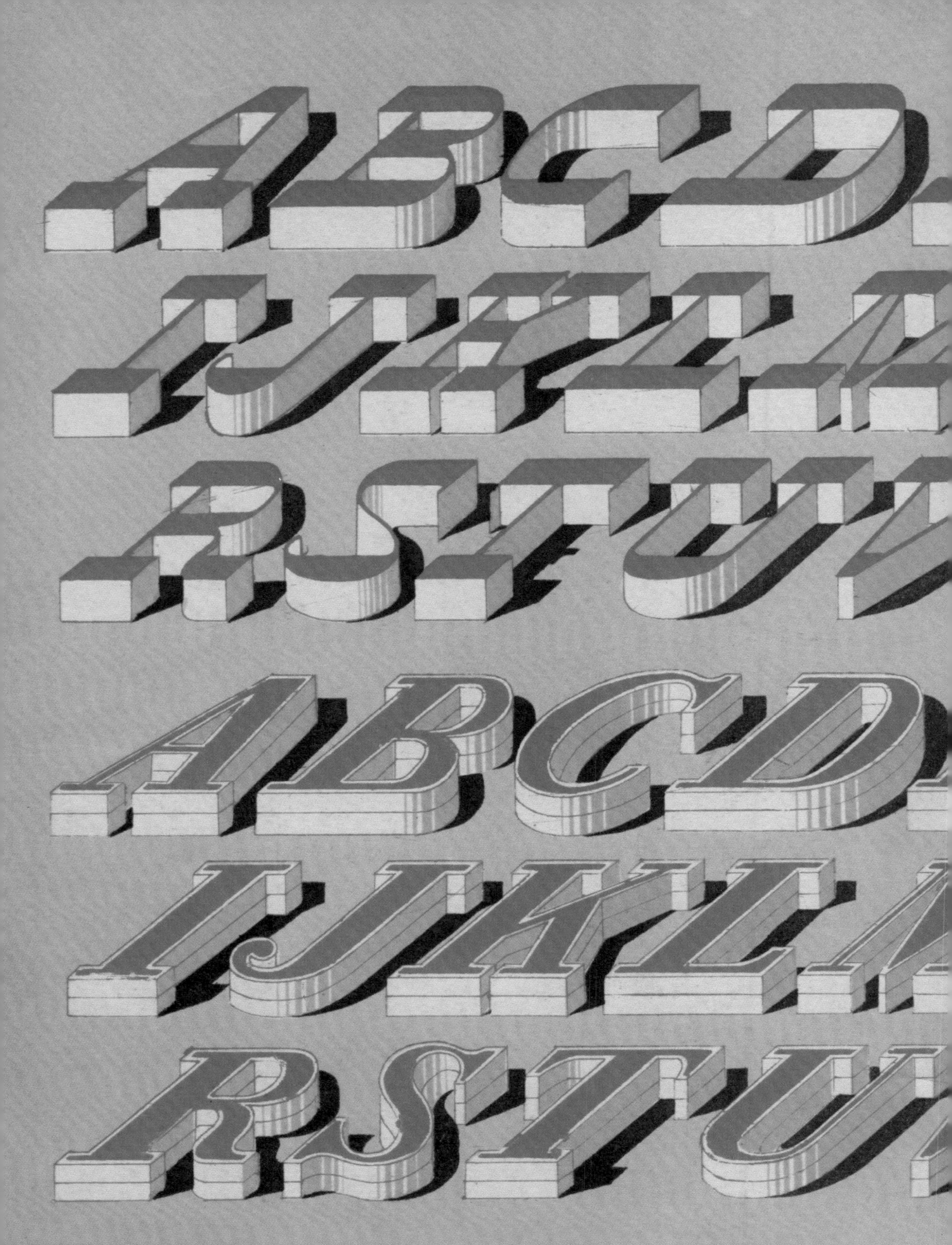

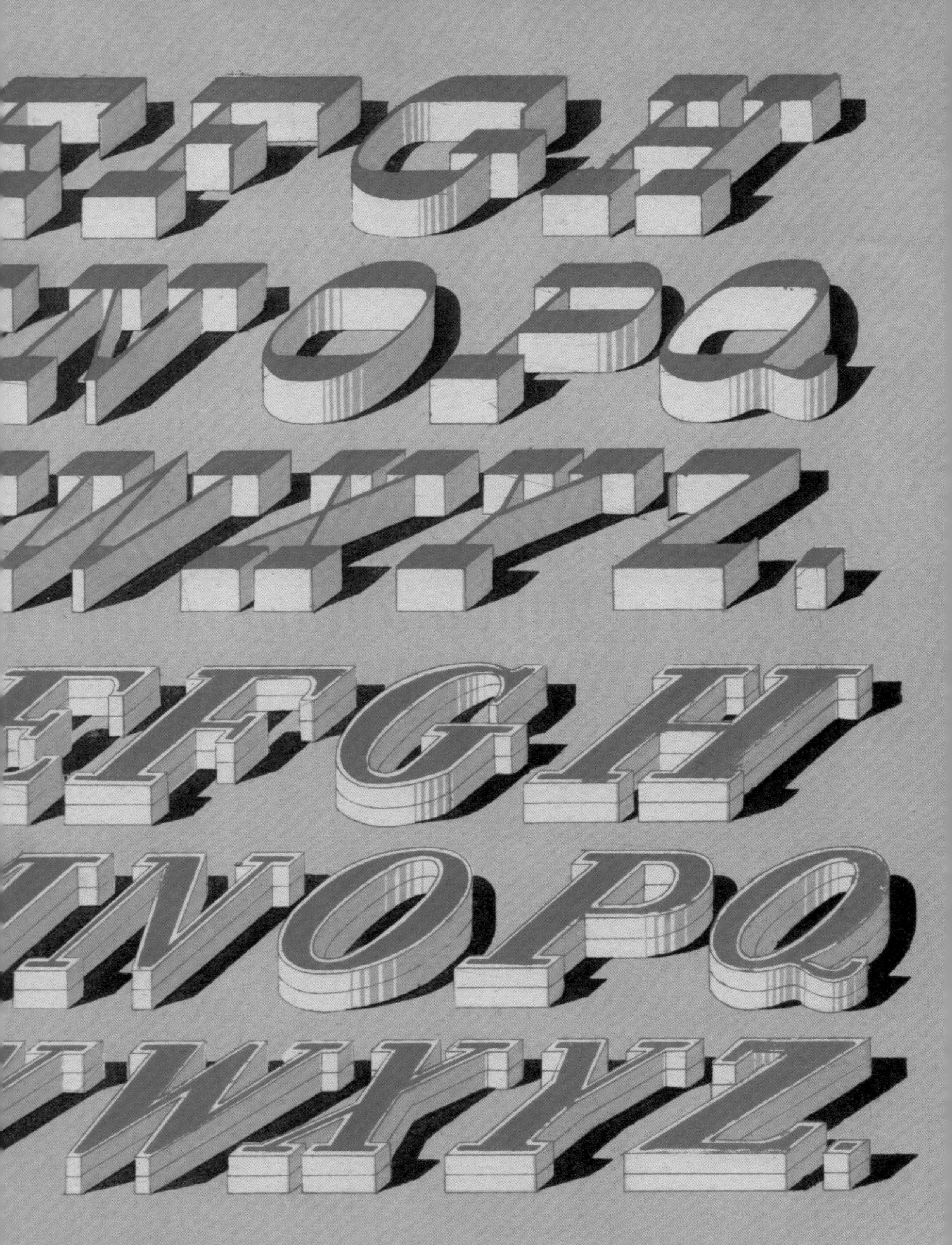

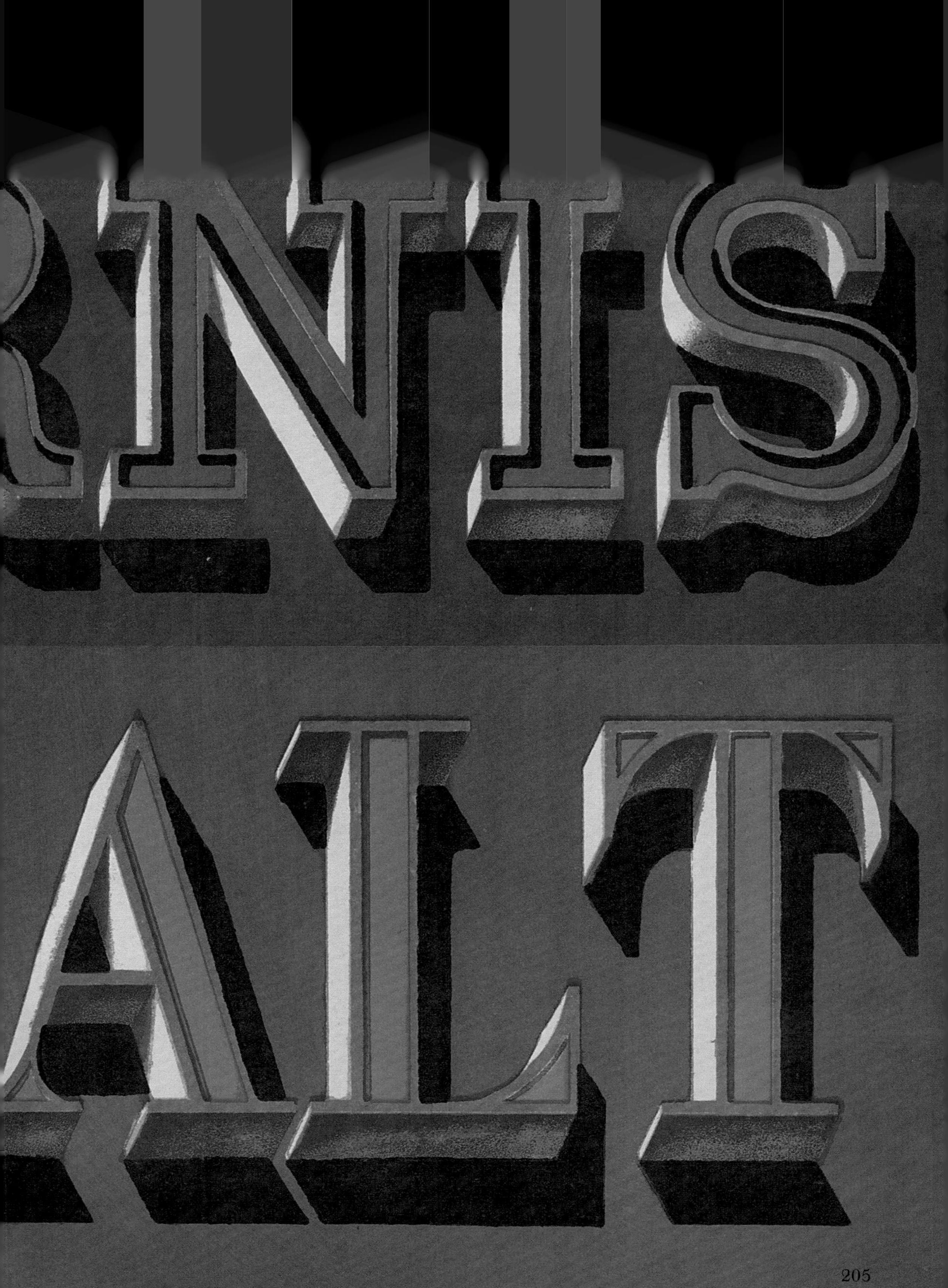
RNIS
ALT

A LA MERE
46
IMPRIMERIE
76
TABLEAUX
VINS & SPIRITUEUX

DE FAMILLE

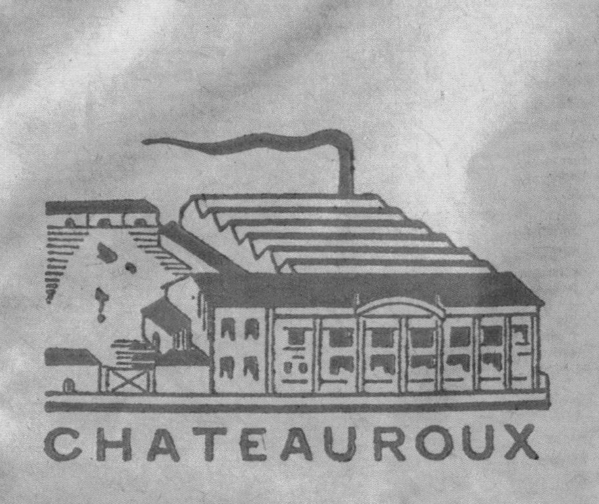
CHATEAUROUX

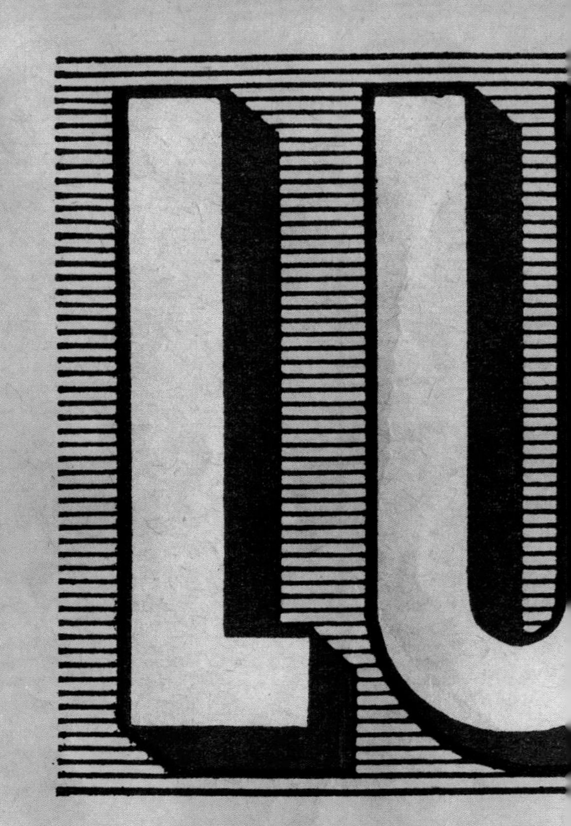
LU

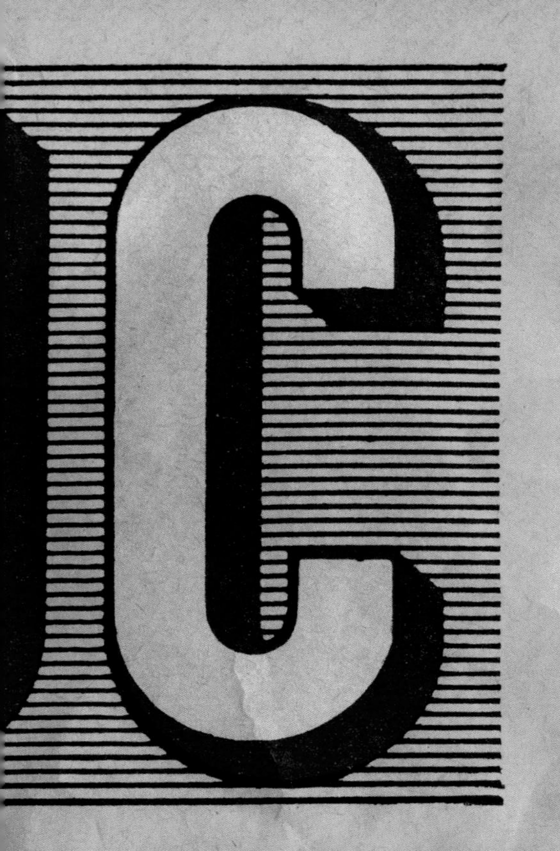

RGAZ

le Rouge"

PROPANE

LA PRÉ

Compagnie d'Assura

Contre les Accide

SOCIÉTÉ ANONYME AU CAPITAL DE

FONDÉ

LU

PETIT-BEURRE

NANTES

GRAND PRIX :: PARIS 1900

LE MEILL

PETIT

LEFÈV

VOYANCE

es à Primes Fixes

de toute nature

MILLIONS ENTIÈREMENT VERSÉS

1864

ONNEMENT À L'ENREGISTREMENT
LOI
du 29 Juin

s'impose ap

Steinhäger

rès la Bière

PRUN
Négociant-Propri

S D'ENTE
A. CHA
caire
A FONGRAVE-SU

Huile d'Olive

Nice

No. 517

jentiane

Suze
Gentiane

SUZE

LLERIE DE LA SUZE

SUZE

SUZE

'AMIE DE L'ESTOMAC

7e ANNEE 1926
MARS N° 3

FRANCE .. 6 fr.
ETRANGER 8 fr.

L'AMOUR DE L'ART

Coulon

LIBRAIRIE DE FRANCE
110, Boulevard Saint-Germain, PARIS

N° 975

Fin
me
Levant
avon
Cologne
du Familistère
PAIN

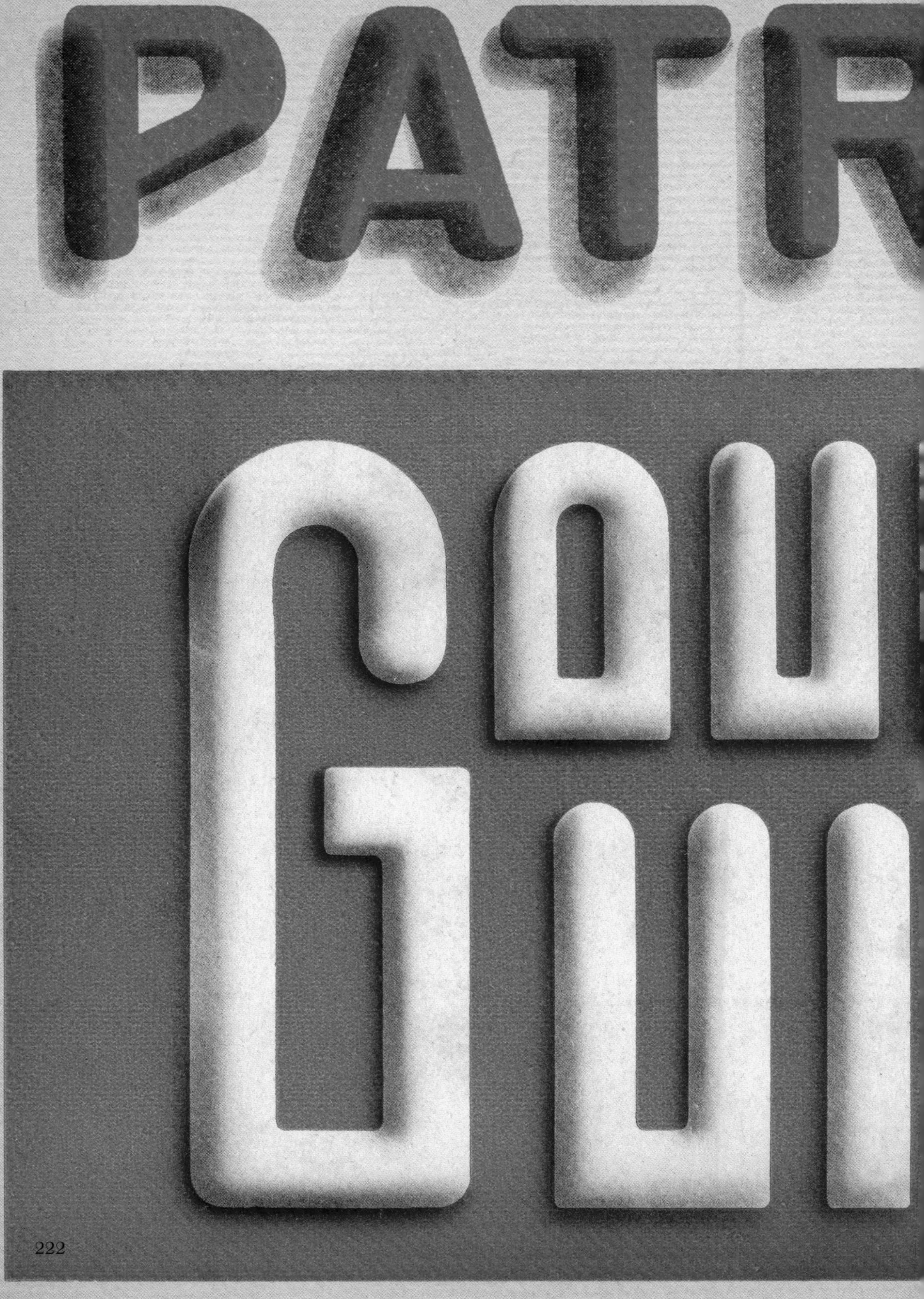

ELLE

ORON

LLOT

LESS

A TUBE INJE

DÉMO

NATI

IEUSE

UR CENTRAL

ABLE

NALE

LES BOULE

"AKA

CA

ESCU

Reconnus

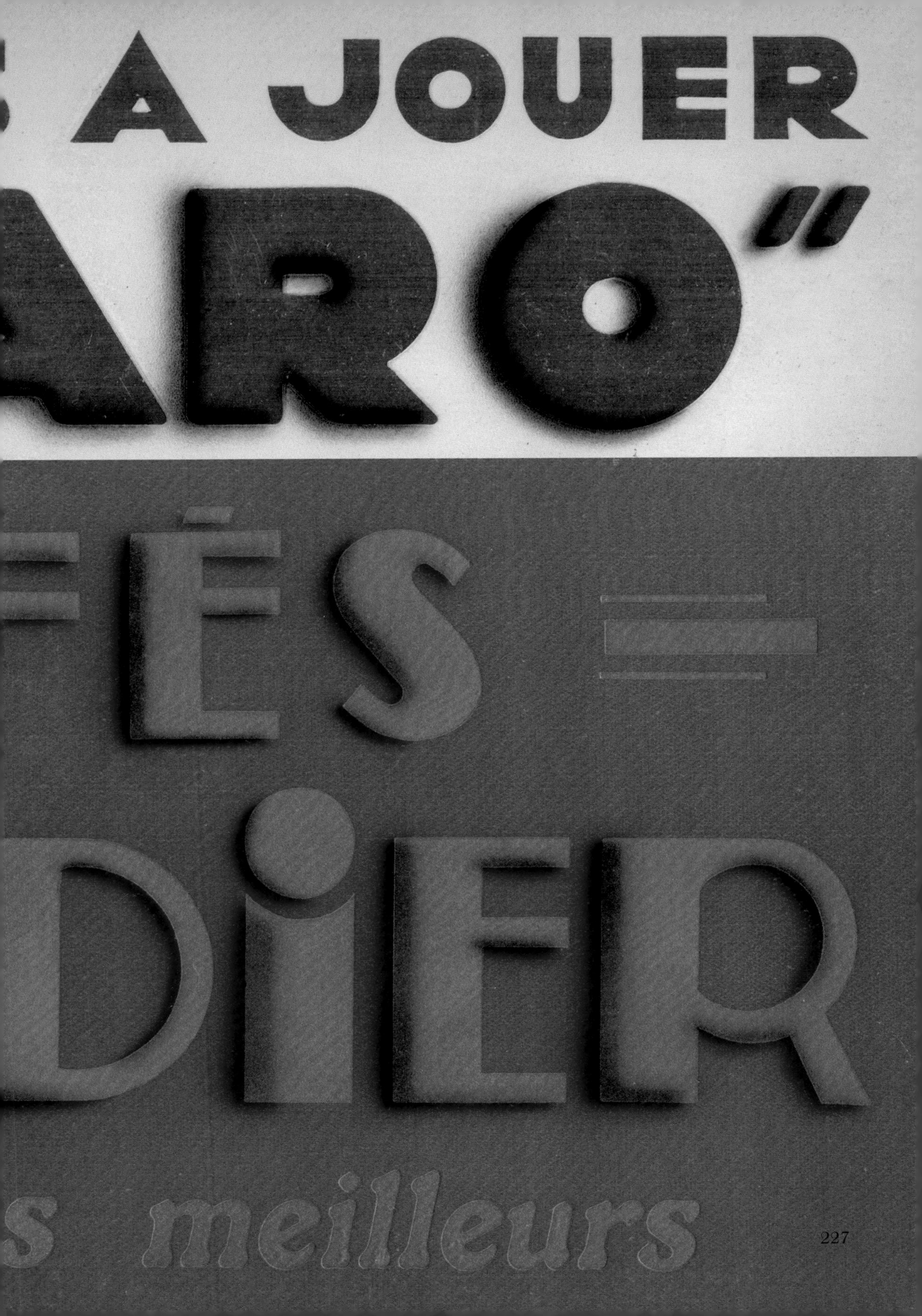

S A JOUER

ARO"

ÉS

DIER

s meilleurs

IN ET AGRÉABLE AME

PICON

CALMODER
DE LA
PEAU
HYGIENE E
BEAUTE DE LA PEA

PROTÈGE EFFICACEMENT
LAINAGES ET FOURRURES

mardi 18 janvier
au
bon m

et jours suivants

arché

ABCD
ABCDEF
GHIJKL
STUV

FGHI
MNOPQR
STUVW
XYZ-
XYZ

La
LETTRE
Relief
ÉLÉMENT
Graphique
DE LA
DECoration
MODERNE

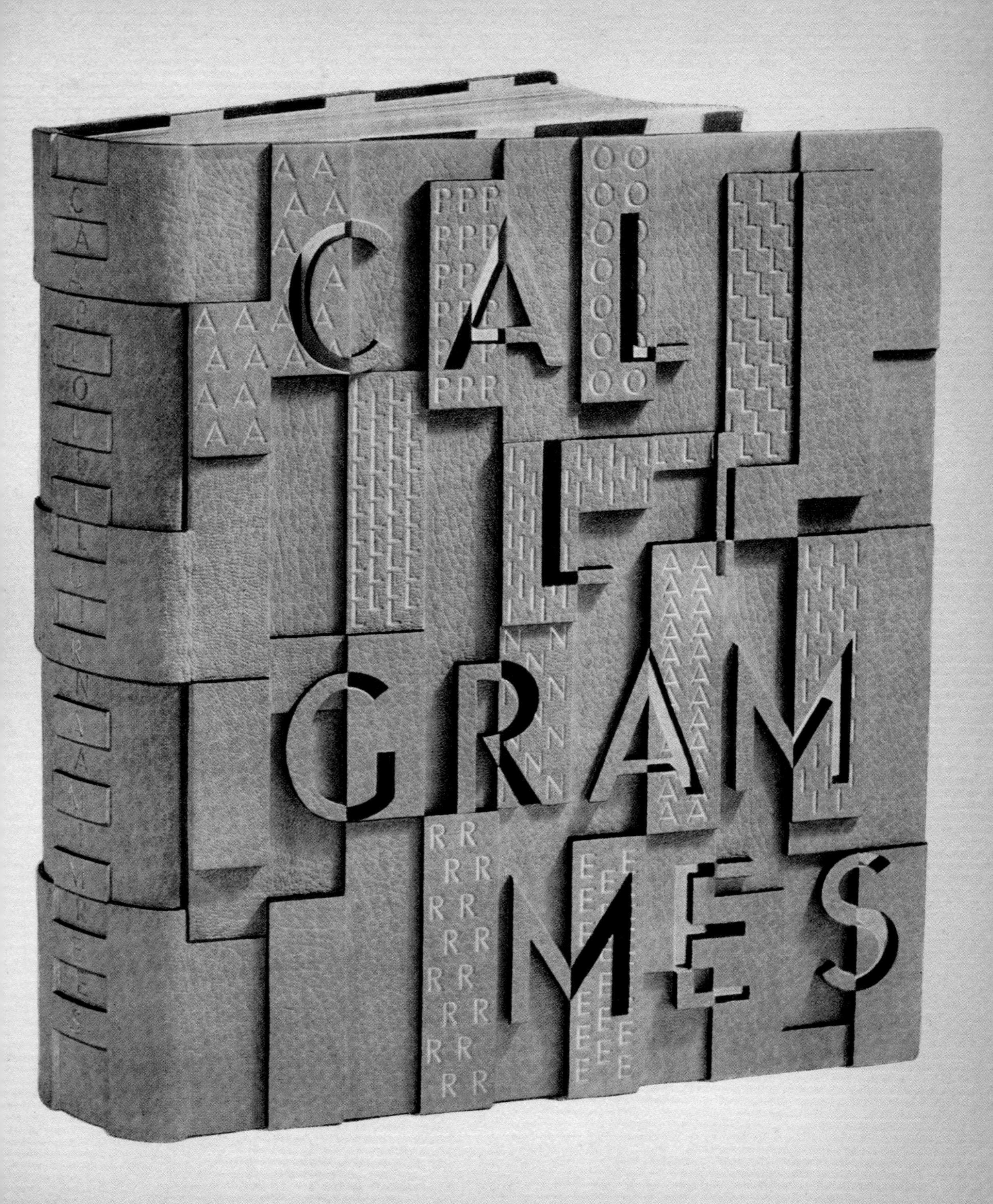
CAL
LI
GRAM
MES

PHOTO

THONET

THONET

SIROP
ROCHE

FONDERIE TYPOGRAPHIQUE MAYEUR, A PARIS

Allainguillaume & Cie, Successeurs

LA PREMIÈRE REPRÉSENTATION

LA CÉRÉMONIE DU MARIAGE

LA MISÉRABLE

LA NATION

LE BOURREAU

PETIT BOIS

TRAIN EXPRESS

L'ACCUSATION

LA LUNE DE MIEL

LA GLOIRE NATIONALE

FRANÇOIS RABELAIS

LE CANAL DE SEINE-&-OISE

FONDERIE TYPOGRAPHIQUE MAYEUR

Allainguillaume & Cie, Successeurs

RENARD ET RAISINS

DOMAINES DE LA PATRIE

LES MODES DE PARIS

DE LA FONTAINE

MÉNESTREL

MUTUELLE

L'UNION

LES PERLES

FRONTIGNAN

ROMAN D'UN HOMME

PRISE DE PEKIN

LE TREMBLEMENT

BET

PUBLICITÉ

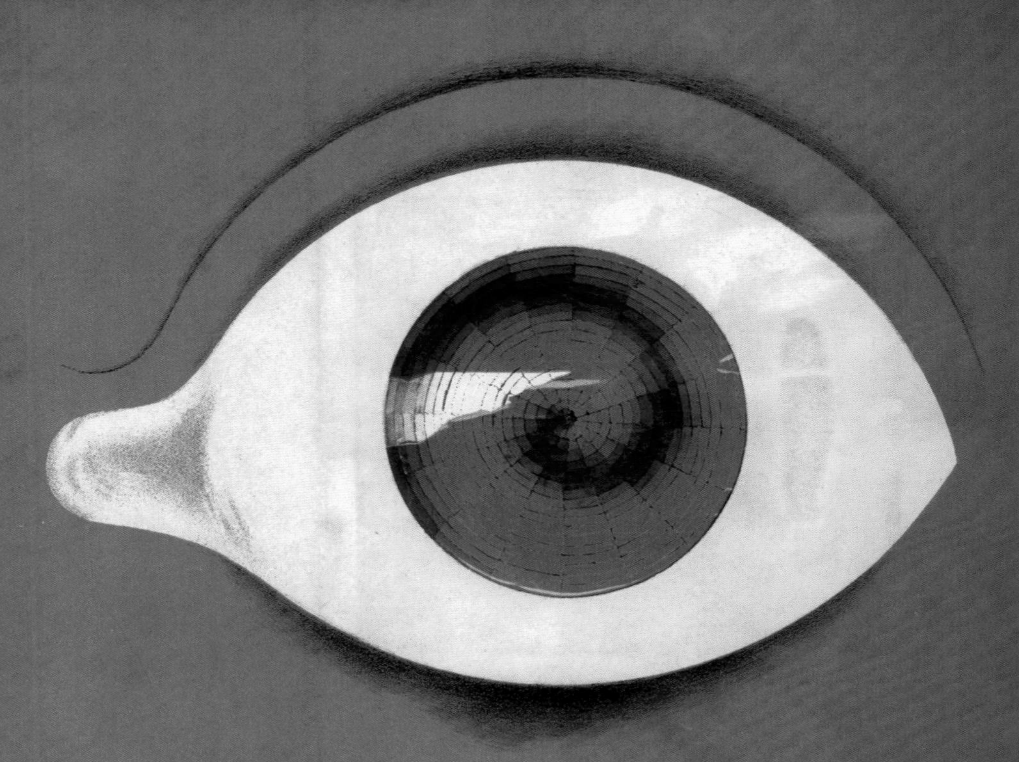

1936

ARTS ET MÉTIERS GRAPHIQUES

COUVERTURE DE JEAN CARLU

HEMOSTYL
DU Dr ROUSSEL

ART

et Industrie

III

LE NUMÉRO : 150 FRANCS

IODIQUE DES ARTS ET DE LA DÉCORATI

VU

ILLUSTRÉ DE LA SEMAINE

21
MARS
1928

KIN
SERVIR TRÈS FROID
APÉRITIFS
GIRONDE
DEMANDEZ
LE PRÉFÉRÉ DES

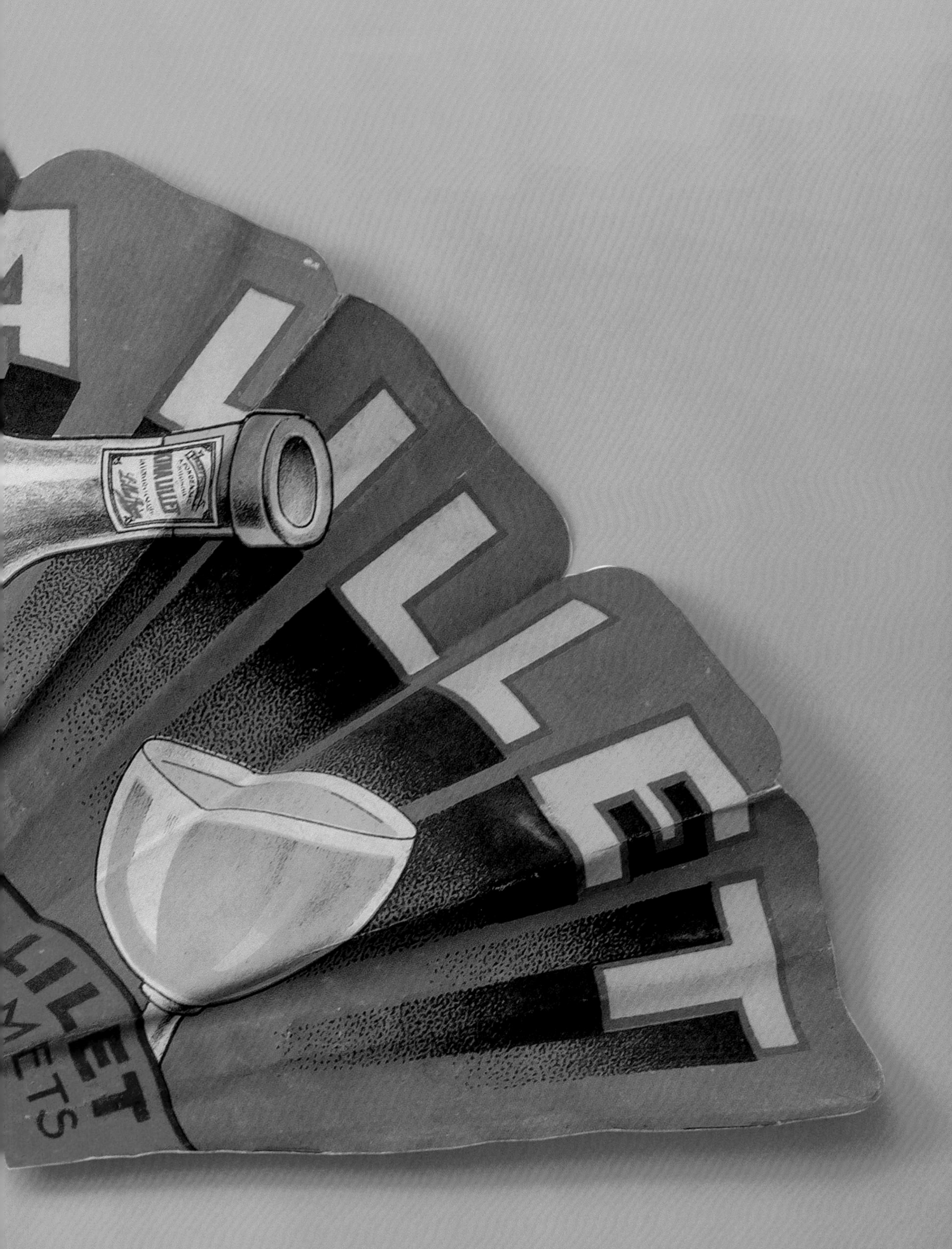
METS

ETAL

AGES

A - MANERA

GAUFRETTES

PAILLE

MARQUE DÉPOSÉE

D'OR

FRAMBOISE

183. Advertisement for "Film" typefaces by Deberny et Peignot, 1932.

184–85. Specimen pages for Floride by Deberny et Peignot and other 19th-century types, undated.

186–205. Specimen pages of sign paintings from *Modèles de Lettres*, 1884.

206–7. Hand-painted and tiled signs in Paris, photographs by Louise Fili.

208–9. Labels for Luc and Antargaz, *c.* 1948.

210–11. Billhead for La Prévoyance insurance, *c.* 1918; sign for Lu biscuits, 1930s.

212–13. Sign for Crick gin, 1940s.

214–15. Wrapper for Prunes d'Ente, *c.* 1919.

216. Label for olive oil from Nice, *c.* 1925.

217. Brochure cover for Suze digestive medicine, *c.* 1932.

218. Cover art for De Marlieu chocolates, 1930s.

219. Cover of *L'Amour de l'Art* magazine, *c.* 1926.

220–21. Labels for scented soap, 1920s.

222–23. Point-of-purchase display cards, *c.* 1930.

224–25. Package label for copper tubing, 1940s.

226–27. Cardboard signs, *c.* 1930.

228–29. Promotional paper lantern for Amer Picon aperitif, *c.* 1930.

230. Point-of-purchase sign for Calmoderm skin cream, 1928.

231. Point-of-purchase sign for O.Z. insect repellent, 1928.

232–33. Advertisement for a Bon Marché sale, 1930s.

234–35. Decorative alphabets from *La Lettre Artistique & Moderne*, 1929.

236. "La Lettre Relief Element Graphique de la Decoration Moderne," date unknown.

237. Limited edition binding for *Calligrammes* by Apollinaire, date unknown.

238–39. Advertisements from Deberny et Peignot, *c.* 1928.

240. Catalog cover for Thonet chairs, 1929.

241. Advertisement for Sirop Roche, 1928.

242–43. Specimen pages of vintage types from Fonderie Typographique Mayeur, Paris, *c.* 1896.

244–45. Point-of-purchase sign for Olibet, 1927.

246. Advertisement for PMLL, a printing and platemaking service, 1933.

247. Cover of the "Publicité" issue of *Arts et Métiers Graphiques* magazine, 1936.

248. Brochure cover for Hemostyl, 1948.

249. Cover of *Art et Industrie* magazine, date unknown.

250–51. Advertisement for *Vu* magazine, designed by A.M. Cassandre, 1928.

252–53. Promotional fan for Kina Lillet vermouth, 1930.

254–55. Cover of the "Etalages" issue of *Arts et Métiers Graphiques* magazine, 1936.

256. Sign for Lu biscuits, *c.* 1925.

GERMAN

UNTIL THE EARLY 20TH CENTURY, THE MOST POPULAR German typefaces were variations on Blackletter (Fraktur, Schwabacher, Textualis, Rotunda), the Gothic style used in Gutenberg's 15th-century Bibles and centuries later promoted by the Nazis as the *Volkschrift* (people's type)—the politically correct alternative to Antiqua (Latin) faces. With the new century, however, came an assortment of more modern typefaces. Called "block letters" for their bold rectilinearity, these included Block, Neuland, and Lo-Type, designed, respectively, by Lucian Bernhard, Rudolf Koch, and Louis Oppenheim. Although they were not originally conceived as dimensional faces, dramatic shadows or highlights were added to the letterforms when required.

Later examples of German shadow lettering were not of the rectilinear, drop-shadow variety so prevalent in the United States and elsewhere in Europe at the time. In the 1920s German typographers introduced a style of "expressionistic" shadows, as seen in the novelty lettering on the cover of *Die Reklame* magazine (opposite). These shadows were the Deco equivalents of the florid tendrils and pistils that had featured heavily in Jugendstil (Art Nouveau) script a few decades earlier.

German foundries did also produce some wildly excessive, ornately flourished designs, however. Decorative designs from the late 19th and early 20th centuries (pp. 260–61) illustrate how a ghosted shadow behind the script could transform flat and conventional types into vibrant and distinctive letterheads. Likewise, a medley of "signatures" from the 1909 *Schriften und Zierat für Anschläge, große Druck-Arbeiten* type catalog (p. 276) demonstrate the way in which two-dimensional letters could be given three-dimensional weight with the addition of contrasting colors.

By the 1930s, dimensional lettering had become a fixture of the German type trade. The cover for *Gebrauchsgraphik* magazine (p. 286), which simulates the look of plaster-made type, is a stunning echo of the typical American-noir title-card treatment (pp. 76–81). Also inspired by film titles, the "1000 Kinos" advertisement (p. 287), which promotes the German movie industry, prefigures the monumental shadow styles seen later on posters for Hollywood blockbusters such as *Ben Hur*.

DIE REKLAME
ZEITSCHRIFT DES VERBANDES DEUTSCHER REKLAMEFACHLEUTE E.V.
V D R
VERLAG FRANCKEN U. LANG G.M.B.H. BERLIN-W30
SONDERHEFT
PACKUNGEN
2. JANUARHEFT 1926
G. SCHAFFER
CHEMNITZ

Schönstes Skigelände
des Vogtlandes

Wintersportplatz

Feinstes Haus am Platze, Bes.:

 ZIMMER MIT ELEKTR.
LICHT UND HEIZUNG

uftkurort-Schöneck

Pension
illa Waldesruh"

21

il Ludwig's Erben

Normal-Mass
Otto Parcus
Quirin Reiner
Südfrüchte & Thee.
Ulrich Vormund.
Wilhelm Xaver Zeitblom

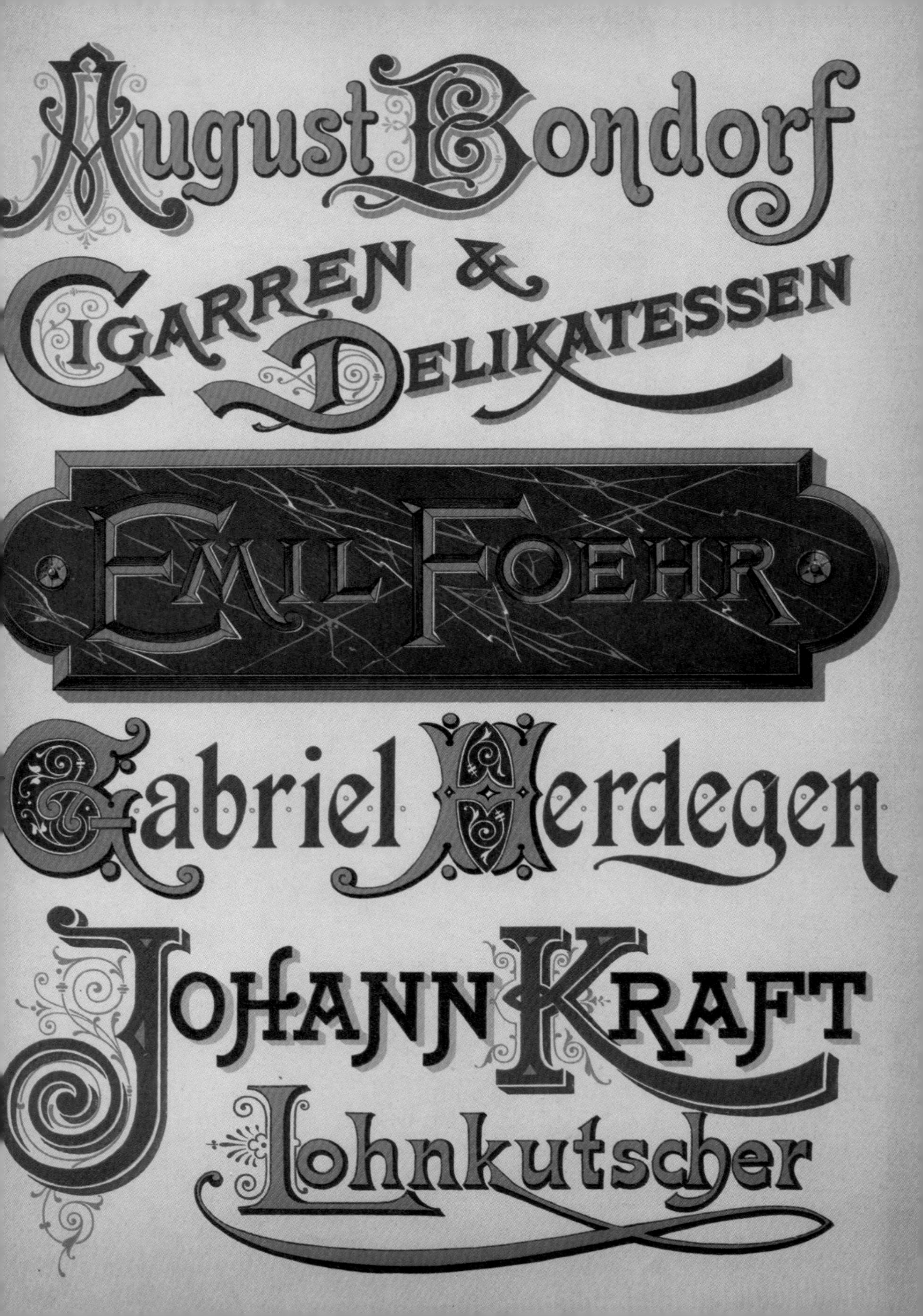

August Bondorf
Cigarren & Delikatessen
Emil Foehr
Gabriel Herdegen
Johann Kraft
Lohnkutscher

Aa Bb

Ee Ff

Iij Kk

1 2 3

Cc Dd

Gg Hh

Ll Mm

4 5 6

GH
KL

I M

N O

LM

QR

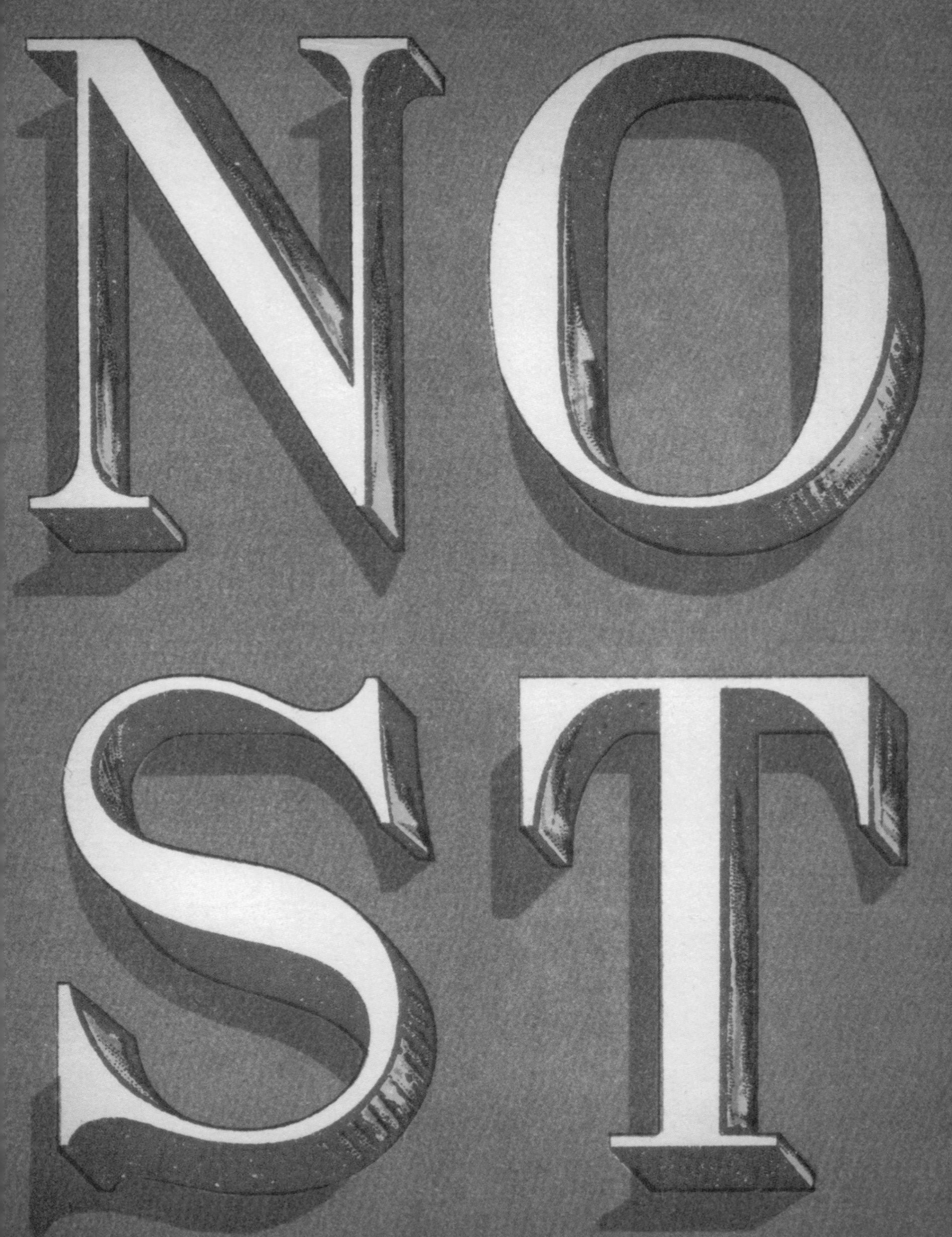
N O
S T

ABCD
JKLM
RSTUV
abcdef
nopqrst
12345

E F G H I

N O P Q

W X Y Z

g h i j k l m

u v w x y z

6 7 8 9 0

STEINHÄGER

ECHT GEBRANNT NACH
DEM ALT-BEWAEHR=
TEN VERFAHREN VON

STEINHÄGERBRENNEREI
STEINHAGEN i.W.
»45 VOL.PROZENT«

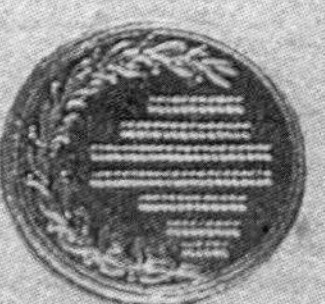

EIN AUS EDLEN TRAUBENWEINEN GEBRANNTER

DEUTSCHER WEINBRAND

Die Reklame

ZEITSCHRIFT DES VERBANDES DEUTSCHER REKLAMEFACHLEUTE E.V.

1. FEBRUARHEFT 1929, HEFT No. 3

VERLAG FRANCKEN UND LANG G.M.B.H./BERLIN W.30

Deutſcher
Ring 1911

Foto
Haus
Rau

Krupp
Dieſel-
Motor

Farben
Pinſel
Lacke!

7

Preise nach Klasse D

Ninive

Blumen

No. 51363. 10 Cicero

Ruben

No. 51365. 12 Cicero

Hoch

No. 51369. 16 Cicero

Mai

No. 51371. 20 Cicero

No. 51364 11 Cic. No. 51366 13 Cic.
No. 51367 14 Cic. No. 51368 15 Cic.
No. 51370 18 Cic. No. 51372 22 Cic.
No. 51373 24 Cic.

Niobe

Preise nach Klasse D

Rund

No. 51375. 10 Cicero

Mur

No. 51379. 14 Cicero

Hilf

No. 51381. 16 Cicero

Ein

No. 51382. 18 Cicero

No. 51376 11 Cic. No. 51377 12 Cic.
No. 51378 13 Cic. No. 51380 15 Cic.
No. 51383 20 Cic. No. 51384 22 Cic.
No. 51385 24 Cic.

J. G. Schelter & Giesecke in Leipzig

A B C D E F
G H I J K L
M N O P Q R
S T U V W
X Y Z a b c
d e f g h i j k
l m n o p q r
s t u v w x

GEBRAUCHSGRAPH

INTERNATIONAL ADVERTISING ART

NOVEMB

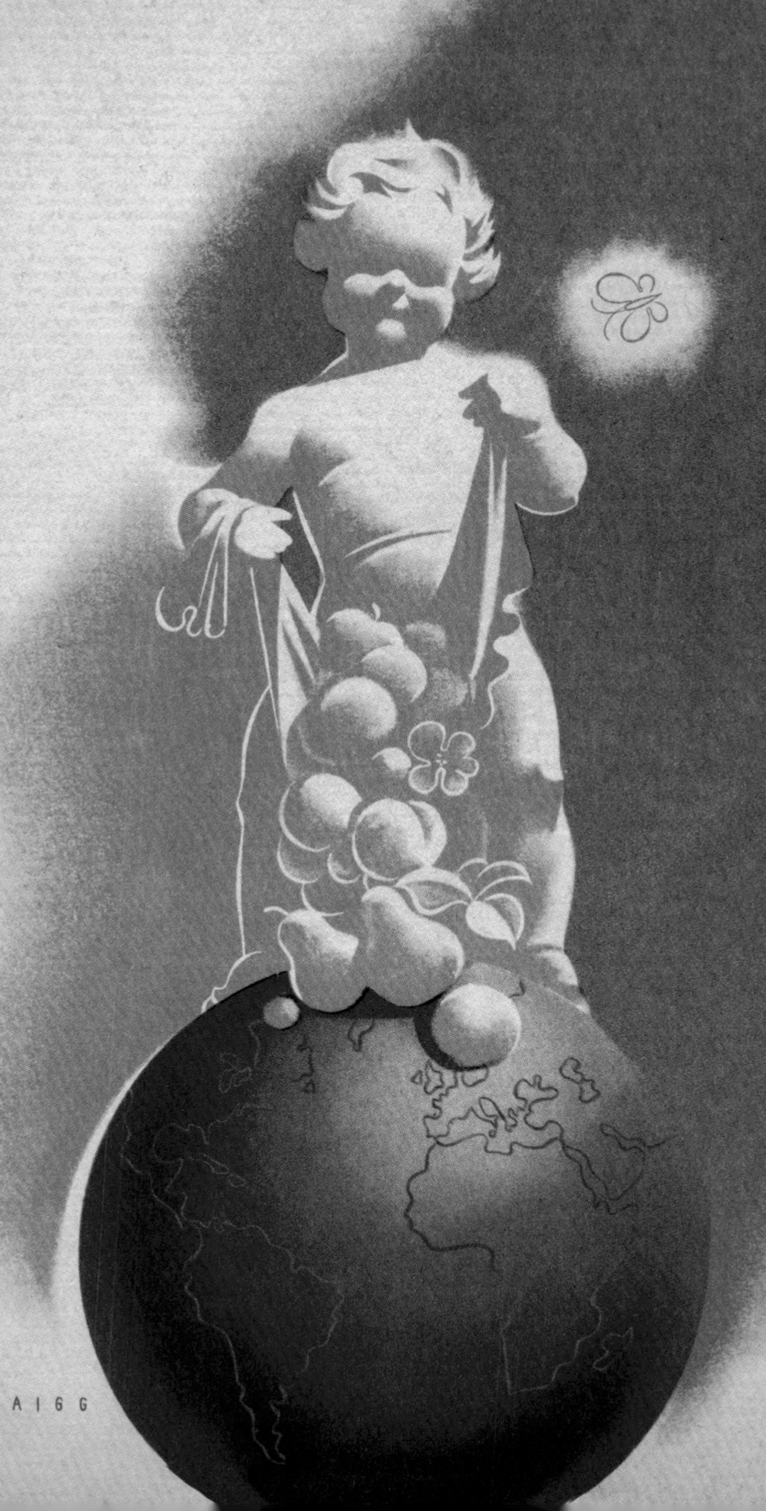

LOIS GAIGG

INTERNATIONAL AD
FRENZEL & ENG
GEBRAUCHSGRAP
BERLIN SW 68, WILHE

ALLEINVERTRETER FÜR U.
THE BOOK SERVI
15 EAST 40th STREET
SOLE REPRESENTAT
UNITED STATES OF AMER

DER
SUMPF
ARMO

DIE
REKLAME
D
V
TSCHRIFT DES DEUTSCHEN REKLAME-VERBANDE
ERBAND DEUTSCHER REKLAMEFACHLEUT

ALMA NACH 1932

S. FISCHER VERLAG

SALTER

as Königsberger Tage

34 Jahrgang

Dienst

930

at

7000

Auflage

as bedeutet

BLECH-EMAILLE-CELL

UNION-WERKE

PLAKATE

LOID-U.GLAS-PLAKATE
G RADEBEUL-DRESDEN
DOSEN

MÄRZ
1934
MARCH
GEBRAUCHS
GRAPHIK
INTERNATIONAL ADVERTISING ART
HERAUSGEBER PROF. H. K. FRENZEL, EDITOR
„GEBRAUCHSGRAPHIK“ DRUCK UND VERLAG GMBH.
BERLIN SW 61, BELLE-ALLIANCE-PLATZ 7-8
ALLEINVERTRETER FÜR DIE VEREINIGTEN STAATEN VON NORDAMERIKA UND KANADA:
THE BOOK-SERVICE COMPANY, SOLE REPRESENTATIVES FOR THE UNITED STATES

1000
KINOS
IM
GANZEN
LAND
FÜR FILMREKLAME
IN EINER HAND

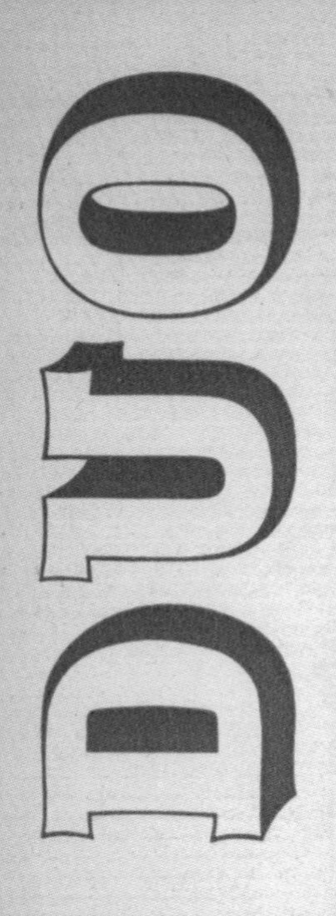

DUO, *die neue einprägsame Versalschrift wird in den Formen „licht" und „dunkel" geliefert. Ihre lebendigen, kraftvollen und ausdrucksstarken Formen geben jeder Drucksache eine sehr nachhaltige Wirkung. Überall dort, wo es gilt ein Wort oder eine Zeile besonders deutlich hervorzuheben, wird diese Akzidenzschrift Verwendung finden.*

ABCDEGHIKMN

Die „zweifarbige Schrift", eine völlig neue Möglichkeit für den Akzidenzsatz, ergibt sich durch den Ineinanderdruck von DUO *„licht" und „dunkel" in verschiedenen Farben, oder bei einfarbigem Druck durch wechselweises Nebeneinanderstellen beider Schnitte.* DUO *„licht" und „dunkel" lieferbar in 20, 28, 36 Pkt. Weitere Grade folgen.*

NEON *Leuchtröhren*

NEON *Leuchtröhren*

NEON *Leuchtröhren*

NEON *Leuchtröhren*

NEDERLAND

SOHUKI.

GFNPZI

HET

LFK

PLATE 18

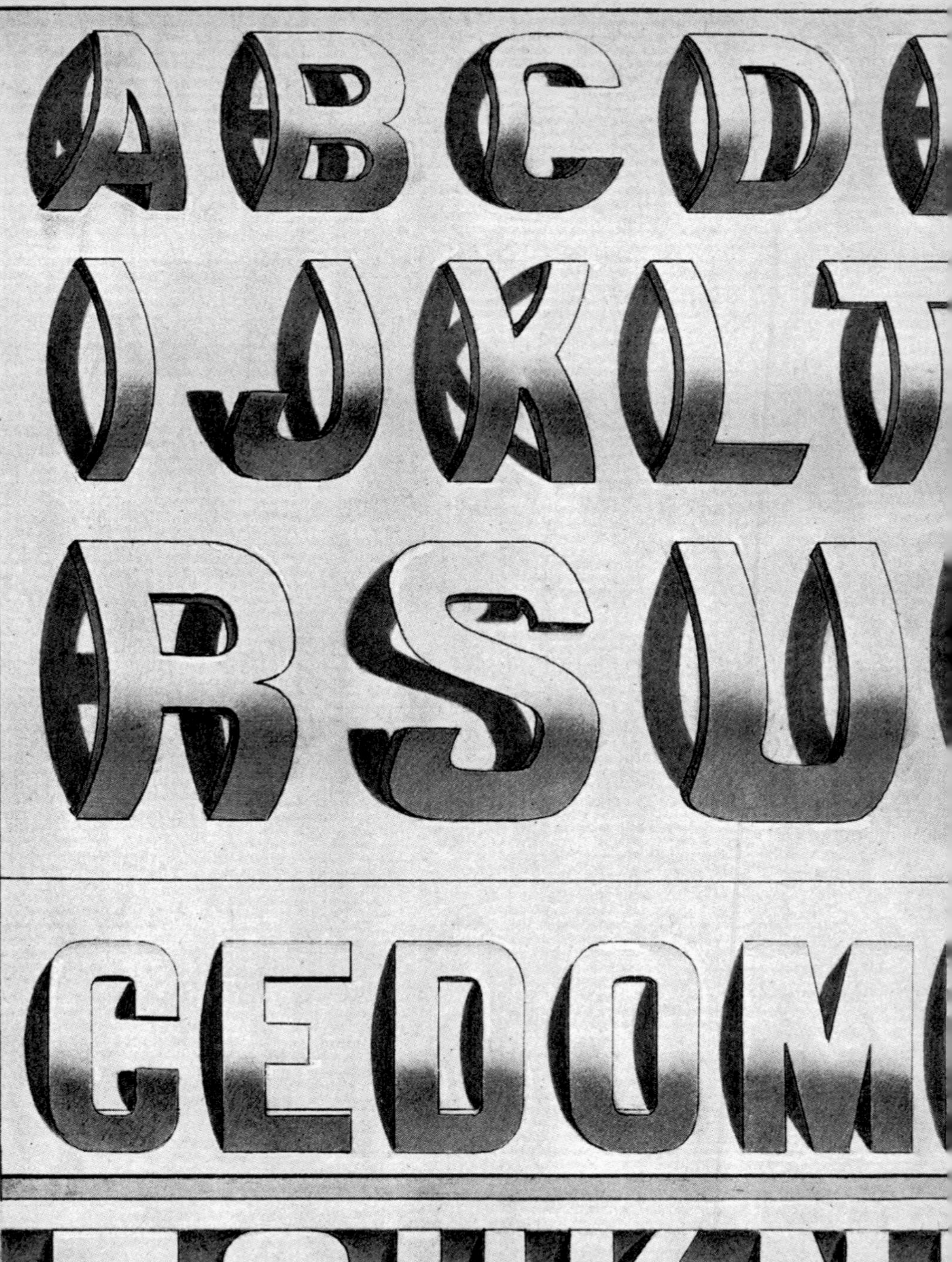

F G H V

M N O P

W X Y Z

U W R A T B

S U V X Z

PLATE 19

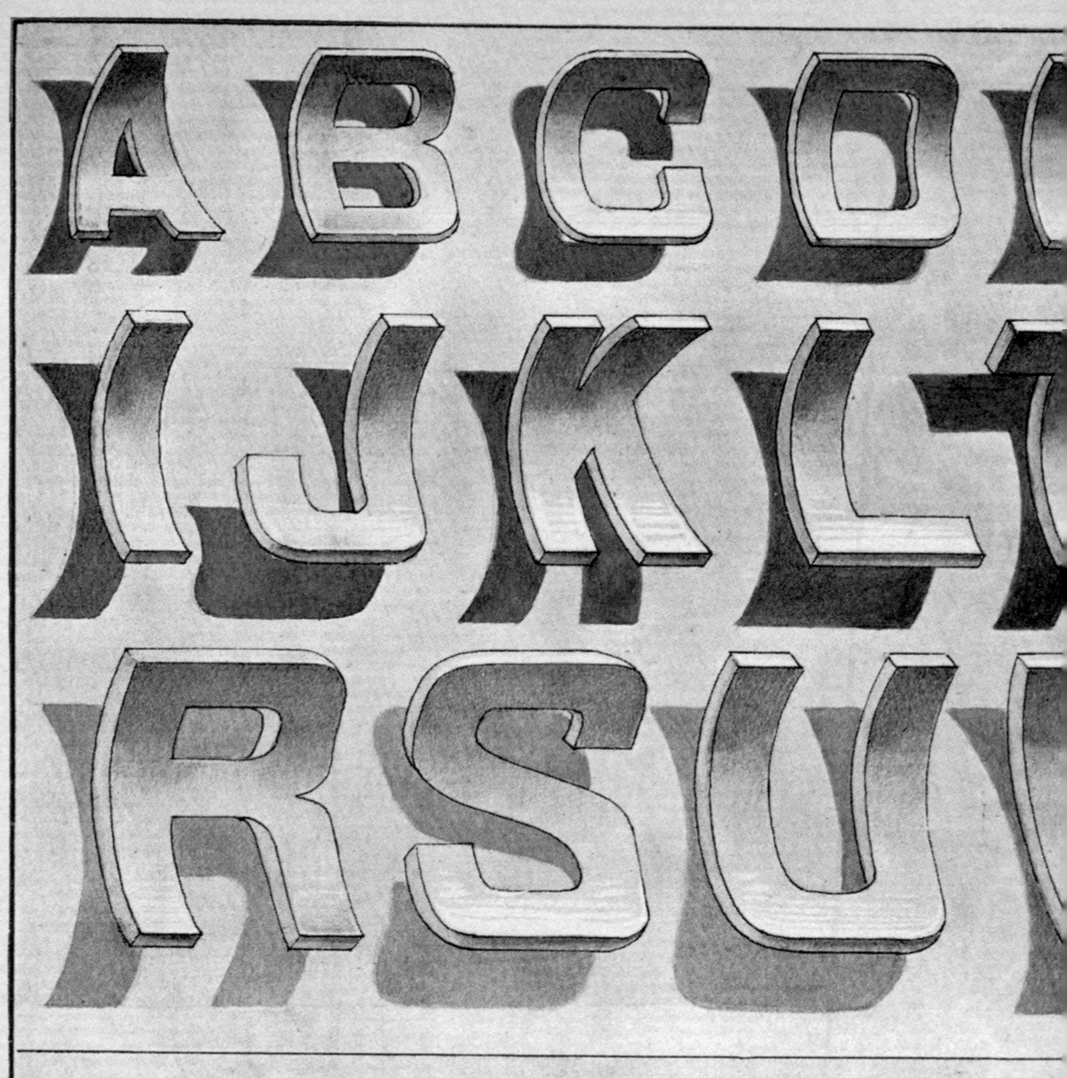

FI

BORDEAU

18

BOEKDRU

DRENTHE

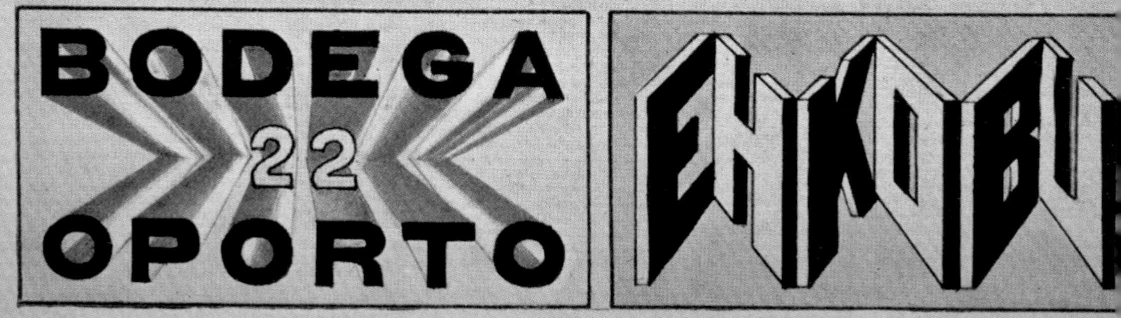

BORDEAU

KKUNST

DRESDEN

RON
SCHI
WMI

IHEIH
OQUHN
CFEPS
WAVIJM

EHEHI
BOJRG
KLTXZ
Y8HEN

SCH

HELFT

FINAN

KON. N

JK

OST

ET

VS

DER

BOORD

CIEEL

D. DECOR

UIZD NRDOO UB

ERASMUSDRUCK · BERLIN · S 42

ERASMUS
DRUCKE

sind Druckarbeiten
hohen inneren Wertes,
starker werbender Kraft

Erasmusdrucke
wählen heisst:
Handeln nach dem
ökonomischen
Prinzip

THANNHAEUSER

259. Cover of *Die Reklame* magazine, designed by G. Schaffer Chemnitz, 1926.

260–61. Letterheads, 1920 and 1925.

262–71. Customized specimen pages from J.G. Schelter & Giesecke's *Schriftenatlas*, 1898.

272–73. Labels for Strothmann Steinhäger beer, designed by O.H.W. Haddank, 1930s.

274. Cover of *Die Reklame* magazine, 1929.

275. Advertisement for the "Deutscher Ring" exhibition, 1933.

276. Specimen page from J.G. Schelter & Giesecke's *Schriften und Zeirat für Anschläge, große Druck Arbeiten*, 1909.

277. Specimen page from Hohberg's *Schriften Buch*, 1932.

278. Cover of *Gebrauchsgraphik* magazine, 1938.

279. Advertisement for Weigang printing firm, 1926.

280. Cover of *Der Sumpf* (The Jungle) by Upton Sinclair, designed by John Heartfield for the Malik Verlag, 1928.

281. Cover of *Die Reklame* magazine, 1929.

282. Cover of *Almanach*, designed by George Salter, 1932.

283. Advertisement for the *King Tageblatt* tabloid newspaper, 1930.

284–85. Advertisement for Union-Werke, 1927.

286. Cover of *Gebrauchsgraphik* magazine, 1934.

287. "1000 Kinos," advertisement for movie advertising, 1927.

288–89. Specimen page for Duo and Neon from Bauer Type Foundry, 1948.

290–305. Specimen pages from the Dutch and German versions of *Kaemmerer's Letter Book*, 1911.

306. Advertisement in *Die Reklame* for Erasmus Drucke, a Berlin printing company, *c.* 1929.

BRITISH

LATE 19TH-CENTURY MERCHANT SIGNS ON GLASS AND WOOD, made for the most part by craftsmen rather than type designers, continue to define the British tradition of dimensional lettering. Printed matter, however, was the real workhorse of consumerism. Posters, placards, and bills were the primary advertising medium in Britain from the Victorian era through the 1920s, '30s, '40s, and beyond. The earliest dimensionalization of a Victorian type was probably Fat Face, cast by the celebrated foundry Stephenson Blake, and including Thorne Shaded and Fry's Sans Serif Shaded. When enlarged, another popular Victorian typeface, Figgins Shaded, was visible from long distances.

Lettering was discussed in depth in reviews of the trade. "Communication...is the essential job of all lettering in advertising," wrote Frederick A. Horn in *The Penrose Annual* (1957), "and this imperative function must be achieved untrammelled...by aesthetic consideration." He added that the "infinite diversity of products and services, to be advertised, the countless variations of media in press and print, and the income groups, age groups and occupational groups to which the advertising may be addressed, ensure an ample field of opportunity for the letterer who is aware of the wide range and subtle appeals of the letter-forms at his command." This wide range included the increasingly popular shadow.

Two world wars stimulated a revival of Victorian Grotesques, especially of the more eccentric historical shadow styles. According to Herbert Spencer in the same issue of *The Penrose Annual*, the postwar fashion for 19th-century Egyptians and Clarendons derived from the surfeit of graphic messages issued to the British public in wartime. "In advertising typography and much ephemeral printing, the brisk, forceful qualities of the heavier-weight Egyptians are particularly valuable in dynamic layouts employing contrast of weight or size," Spencer noted, and he could have added dimensionality. By contrast, he decried the 20th-century versions as "anaemic by comparison with their nineteenth century forerunners," labeling them "sickly monstrosities." Luckily for Spencer, the "modern rather sexless sans-serifs" were eclipsed by the range of more forceful dimensional options that dominated the typographic landscape at the time.

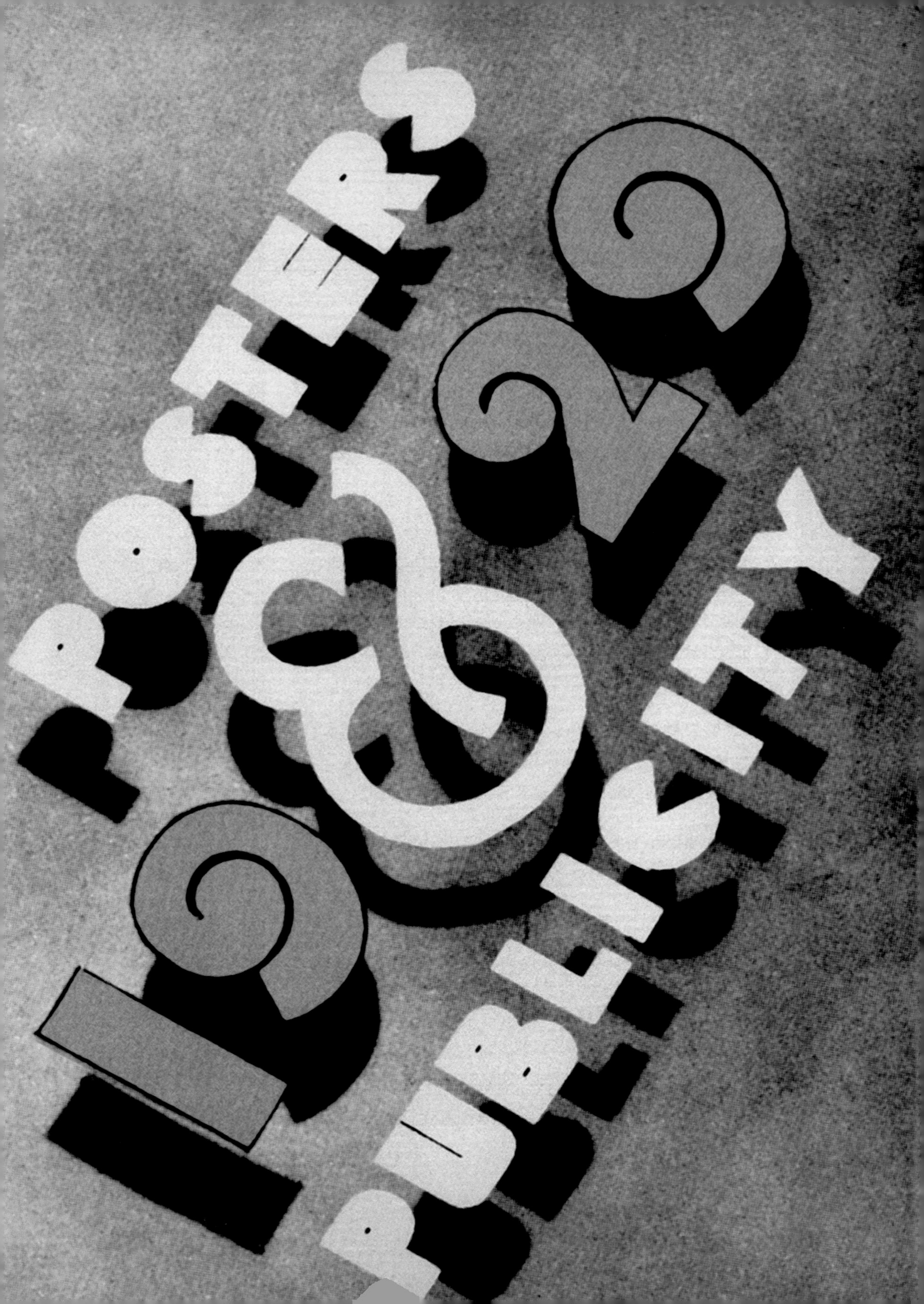
POSTERS
&
PUBLICITY
1929

ALPHABET AND IMAGE

4

SHENVAL PRESS

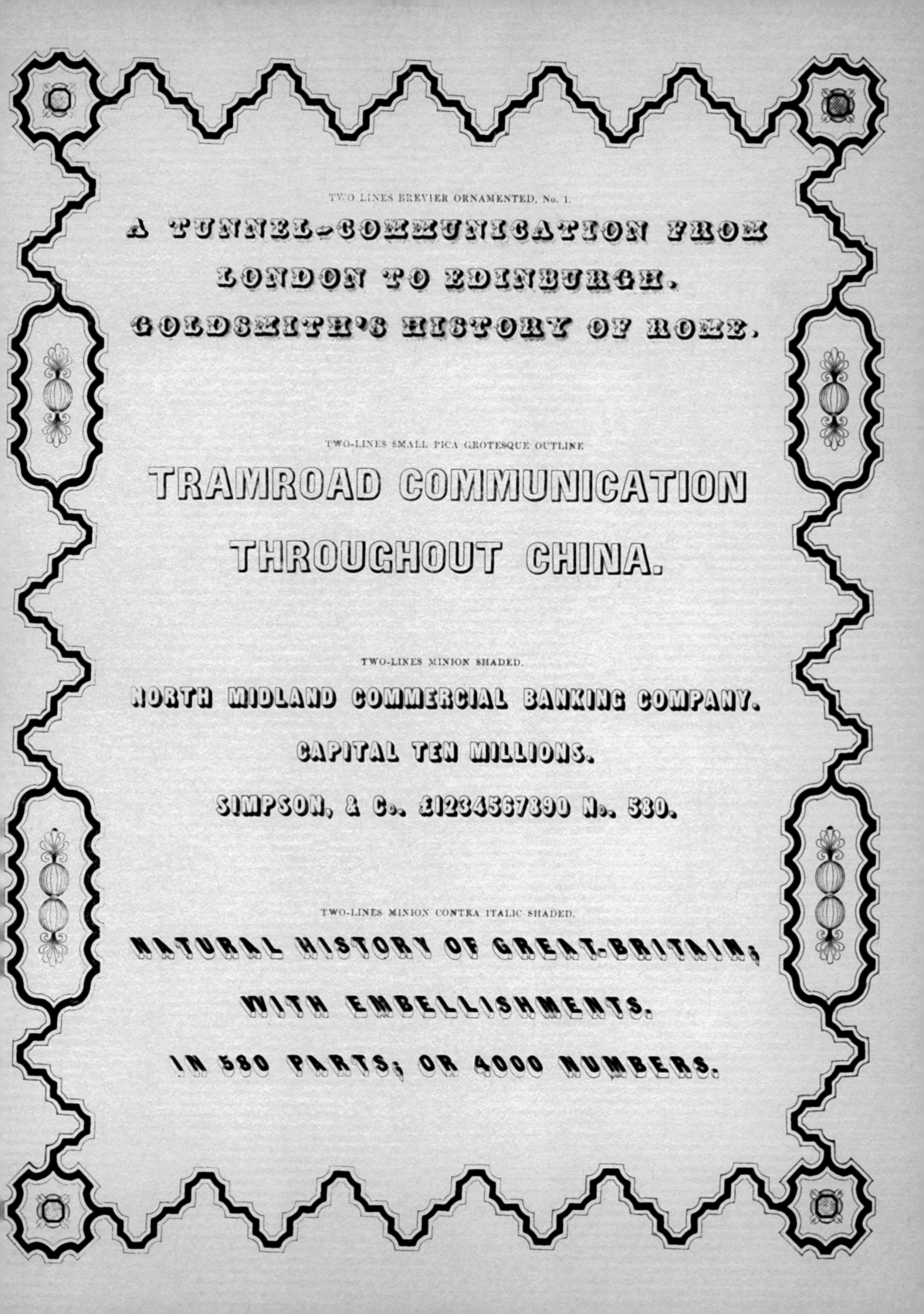

TWO LINES BREVIER ORNAMENTED, No. 1.

A TUNNEL-COMMUNICATION FROM
LONDON TO EDINBURGH.
GOLDSMITH'S HISTORY OF ROME.

TWO-LINES SMALL PICA GROTESQUE OUTLINE

TRAMROAD COMMUNICATION
THROUGHOUT CHINA.

TWO-LINES MINION SHADED.

NORTH MIDLAND COMMERCIAL BANKING COMPANY.
CAPITAL TEN MILLIONS.
SIMPSON, & Co. £1234567890 No. 580.

TWO-LINES MINION CONTRA ITALIC SHADED.

NATURAL HISTORY OF GREAT-BRITAIN;
WITH EMBELLISHMENTS.
IN 580 PARTS; OR 4000 NUMBERS.

WE SHOULD
NOT TRUST IN
OURSELVES,
BUT IN GOD.
2. COR. I. 9

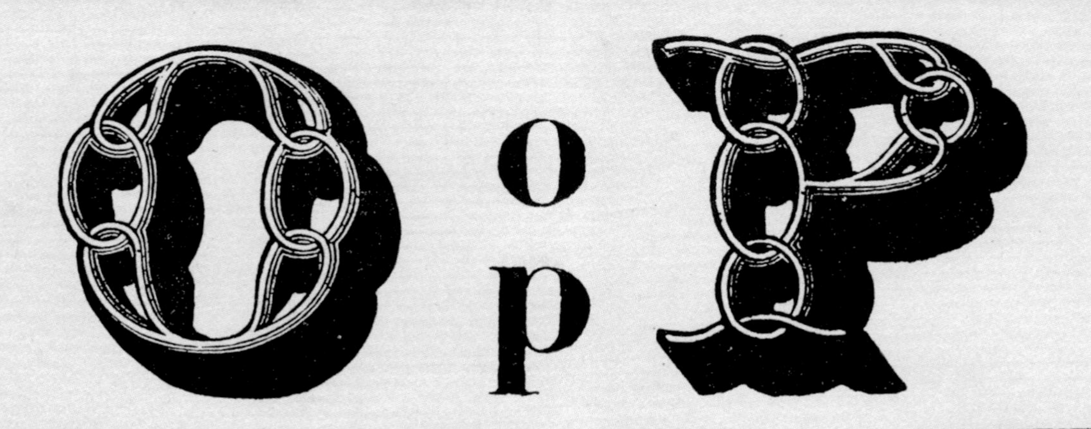

s

t

w

x

DEAN AND SON,

11, LUDGATE-HILL, LONDON.

PHILLIPS

LORENZ

MURIELS

ETHERDO
BAYLEY
CRIS

Dean & Son's

YOUNG CHILD'S OWN ALPHABET.

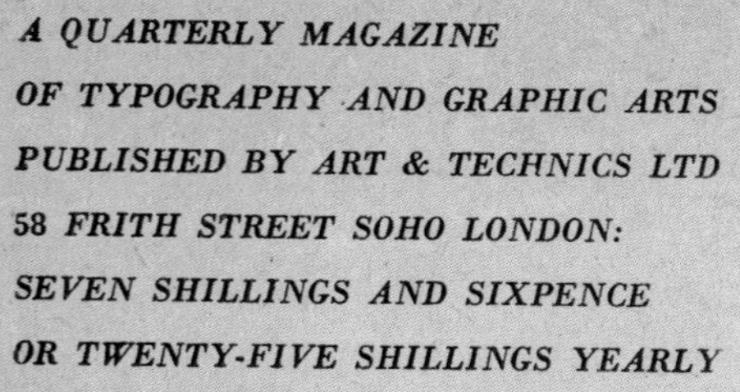
A QUARTERLY MAGAZINE
OF TYPOGRAPHY AND GRAPHIC ARTS
PUBLISHED BY ART & TECHNICS LTD
58 FRITH STREET SOHO LONDON:
SEVEN SHILLINGS AND SIXPENCE
OR TWENTY-FIVE SHILLINGS YEARLY

ALPHABET AND IMAGE

THIS ISSUE CONTAINS ARTICLES ON:

TWENTY FOUR LINES SHADOW SANS (for One Colour)

HIN

FOURTEEN LINES SHADOW SANS (for One Colour)

MINE

TEN LINES SHADOW SANS (for One Colour)

INSURE

OTHER SIZES SUPPLIED WITH EQUAL FACILITY

SIXTEEN LINES SHADOW SANS (for One Colour)

DUG

TWELVE LINES SHADOW SANS (for One Colour)

MENU

EIGHT LINES SHADOW SANS (for One Colour)

BRIGADE

SIX LINES SHADOW SANS (for One Colour)

ALPHABETS

OTHER SIZES SUPPLIED WITH EQUAL FACILITY

STEPHENSON, BLAKE & CO. LIMITED

SHEFFIELD, LONDON, MANCHESTER

TWENTY LINES SHADOW SANS (for Two Colours)

DIG

FOURTEEN LINES SHADOW SANS (for Two Colours)

HIND

TEN LINES SHADOW SANS (for Two Colours)

DUCKS

OTHER SIZES SUPPLIED WITH EQUAL FACILITY

SIXTEEN LINES SHADOW SANS (for Two Colours)

RICE

TWELVE LINES SHADOW SANS (for Two Colours)

HUNG

EIGHT LINES SHADOW SANS (for Two Colours)

DICKENS

SIX LINES SHADOW SANS (for Two Colours)

LEMONADE

OTHER SIZES SUPPLIED WITH EQUAL FACILITY

SIGNS

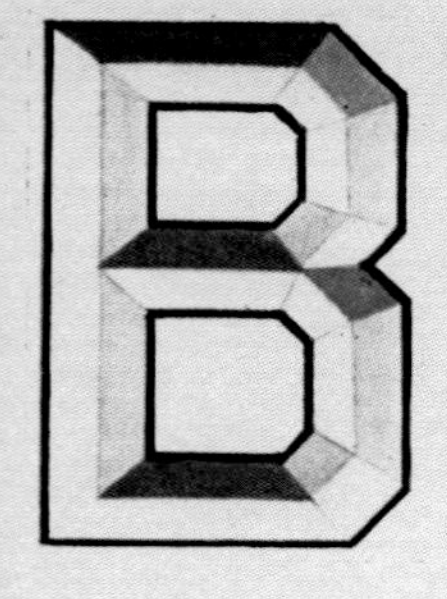

B. 1.
SEGMENT.

B. 2.
ROUND BLOCK.

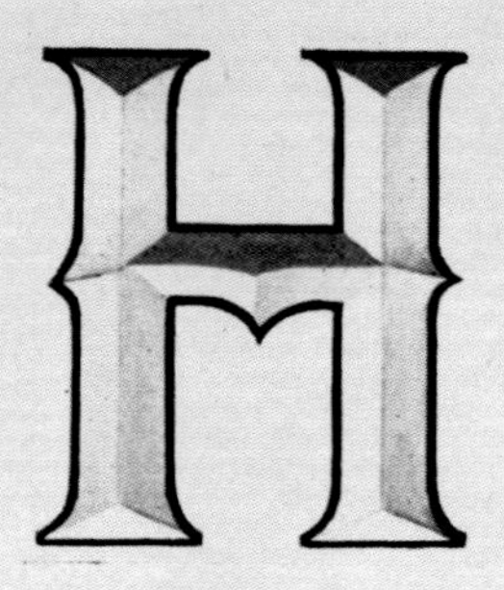

B. 3.
SERIF BLOCK.

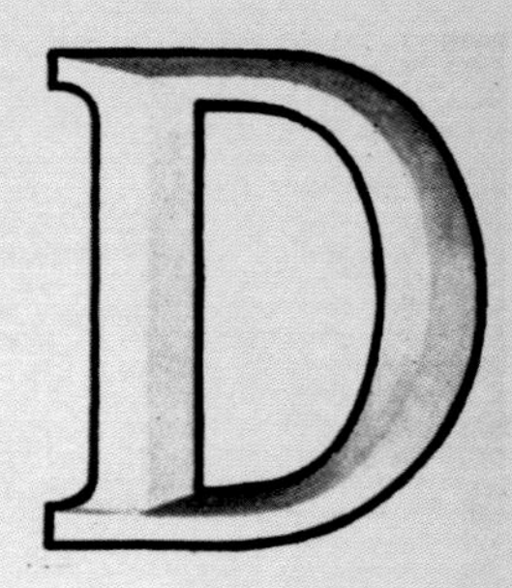

B. 4.
ROMAN.

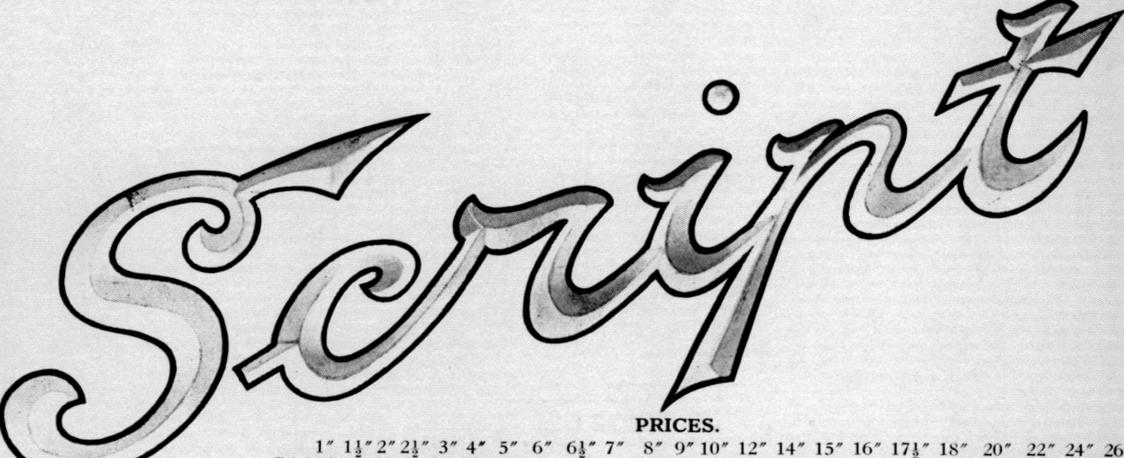

PRICES.

	1″	1½″	2″	2½″	3″	4″	5″	6″	6½″	7″	8″	9″	10″	12″	14″	15″	16″	17½″	18″	20″	22″	24″	26″
B 1-2	3d	4d	5d	6d	7½d	10d	1/1	—	1/3	—	1/8	—	3/6	4/10	—	5/10	—	—	8/6	11/8	14/4	16/10	20/6
B 3	—	5d	7½d	—	10d	1/2	1/6	1/10	—	—	2/6	—	4/4	6/-	7/-	—	10/6	—	—	14/6	—	—	—
B 4	—	—	7½d	8½d	10d	1/2	1/6	—	—	2/-	—	3/6	—	6/-	7/-	—	10/6	—	—	14/6	—	—	—
B 6	—	—	—	—	—	1/2	—	1/10	—	—	2/6	—	4/4	6/-	7/-	—	10/6	—	12/-	14/6	17/6	—	23/-
B 7	—	5d	—	8½d	—	1/2	1/6	—	—	—	—	—	4/4	6/-	7/-	—	—	—	—	14/6	—	—	—
B 8-9	—	—	—	—	1/-	1/6	1/10	2/3	—	—	3/-	—	5/6	7/-	8/6	—	—	14/-	—	—	20/-	—	—

Special prices given for Script Lettering according to size and wording.

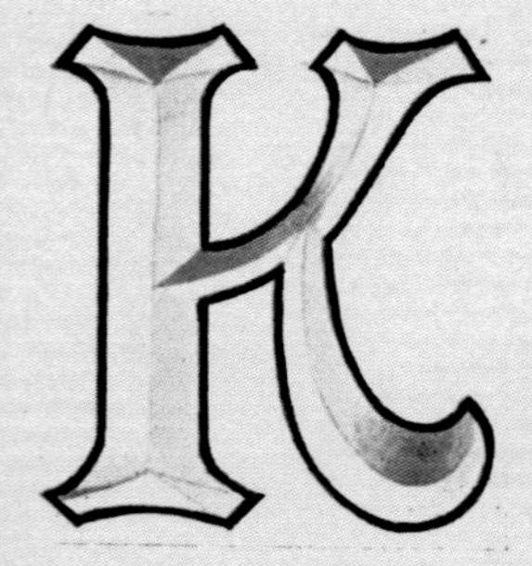

B. 6.
NEW CENTURY.

B. 7.
ARCHITECTURAL.

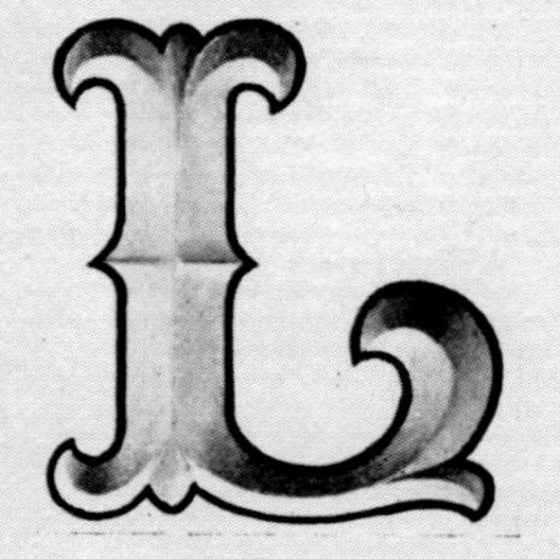

B. 8.
FISHTAIL.

B. 9.
SEMI-FISHTAIL.

WOOD LETTERS. ALL STYLES.

P R H E

W. 60.
FLAT BLOCK.

W. 61.
HALF ROUND.

W. 62.
FLAT SERIF.

W.63.
HALF ROUND ROMAN.

W. 64.

Fancy

We make a special feature of the manufacture of Wood Letters of every conceivable shape and section. Send us your particulars along and we shall be pleased to supply sketches and specifications with prices by return of post.

W. 65.

Types.

W. 66.

W. 67.

W. 68.

W. 69.

G O E H

BEVELLED.

CHAMFERED.

HALF ROUND ON FLAT.

RIBBON.

The Brilliant S

LIANT SIGN CO. LTD.

PECIMENS OF THE LARGEST SIGN ORDER EVER PLAC

VER 50,000 BRILLIANT SIGNS MANUFACTURED

ARAGON WORKS W.12 THE MODEL SIGN WORKS OF THE EMP

GE JUBILEE DISPLAY AT B.I.H. MARBLE ARCH

BRILLIANT SIGN C

BRILLIANT SIGNS

WILLS'S STAR CIGARETTES

WILLS'S CAPSTAN CIGARETTES

WILLS'S WOODBINE CIGARETTES

WILLS'S GOLD FLAKE CIGARETTES

WILLS'S FOUR ACES CIGARETTES

WILLS'S WOODBINES

LLIANT SIGN Co LTD

STANLEY JONES & Co L

ART
AND INDUSTRY...
APRIL 1941. 35 CENTS

ART AND INDUSTRY

35 CENTS
FEBRUARY
1941

THE

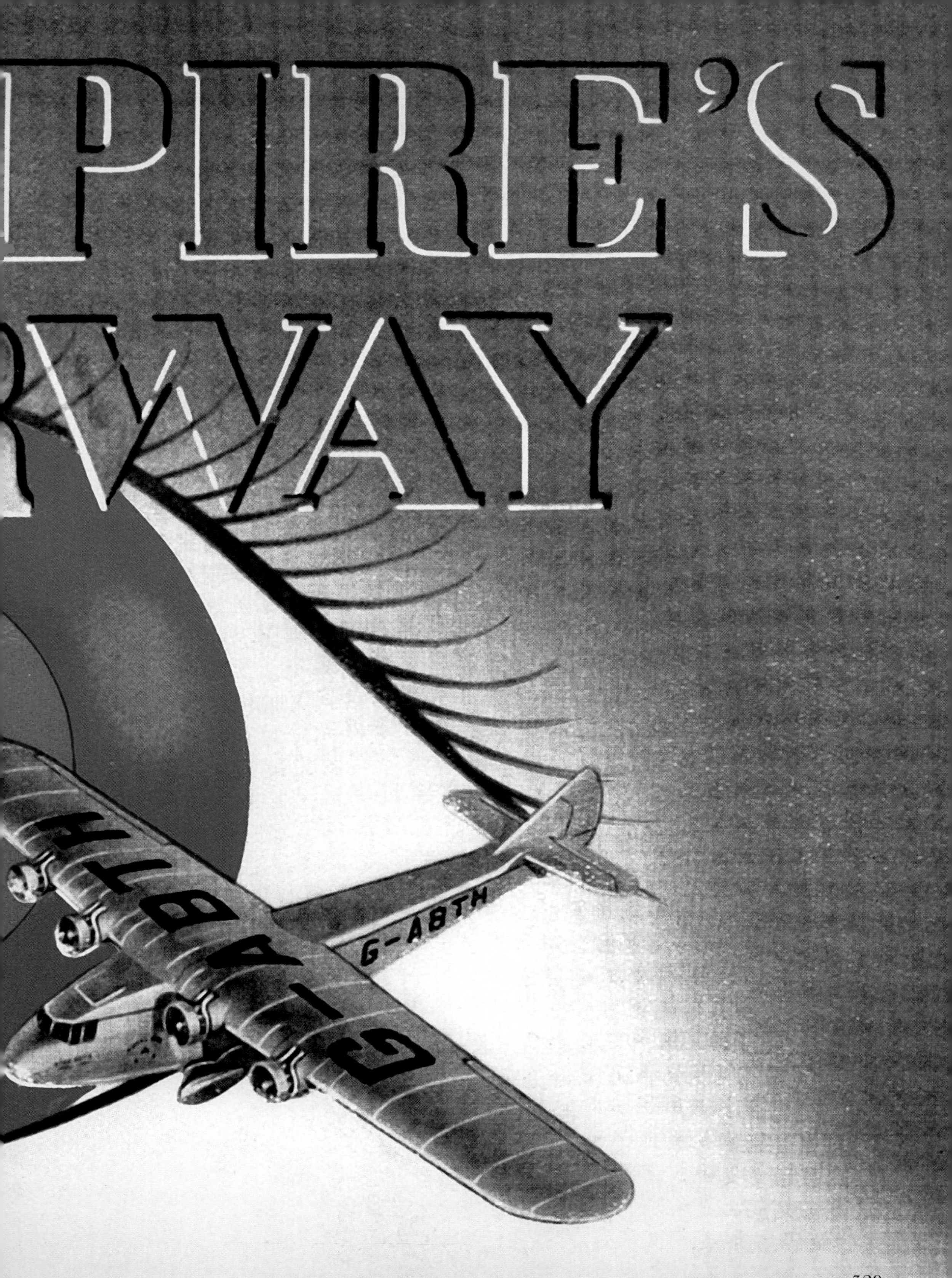

PIRE'S
WAY

FORTNUM
AND
MASON

SPRING 1933
COLLECTION

JAPAN
JAPANESE GOVERNMENT RAILWAYS

AUTUMN 2 1949

a quarterly of the visual arts

IFE SCULPTURE: by William Fagg

THE DRAWINGS OF BEN SHAHN: by Bernarda Bryson

THE TOPOGRAPHICAL DRAWINGS OF JOHN PIPER: by S. John Woods

IMAGES OF MOVEMENT: by Peter Goffin

MR HUTCHINSON'S SPORTIN' VENTURE: by R. A. Bevan

5s

309. Cover of *Posters & Publicity* magazine, 1929.

310. Cover of *Alphabet and Image* magazine, 1947.

311. Specimen page of Brevier Ornamented, Grotesque Outline, Minion Shaded, and Minion Contra Italic Shaded, *c.* 1900.

312–13. Pages from *Alphabet and Image* magazine, 1947.

314–15. Wood type from a poster for the Prince of Wales Theatre, London, 1888.

316–17. Covers of *Alphabet and Image* magazine, 1947.

318–21. Specimen pages of Shadow Sans from Stephenson Blake & Co. Ltd., 1950.

322–23. Pages from the Brilliant Signs Ltd. catalog, 1930s.

326–27. Covers of *Art and Industry* magazine, 1941.

328–29. Cover of "The Empire's Airway" brochure, 1934.

330. Cover of Fortnum and Mason's Spring catalog, 1933.

331. Poster for Japanese Government Railways, 1937.

332. Cover of *Image* magazine, 1949.

MISCELLANEOUS

SHADOW TYPEFACES ARE NOT LIMITED TO THE SMALL NUMBER OF countries we have looked at. All nations with active advertising, packaging, and type industries use them. They have never been banned or censured by governments, nor have they been exalted as typographic masterpieces. They exist simply because they have long served a useful function.

Shadows are familiar stylistic devices in commercial typographic environments because they are so versatile. They can be simple or elaborate, depending on how the shadow is applied and in what context it is used. Indeed, adding a shadow can lend sophistication to a plain typeface, yet make a more complicated style look overdone—like adding too much eye-shadow or blush to the human face.

Some dimensional letters are classics while others are novelties, although arguably the majority are used as one-offs. Over time, the popularity of shadow type has fluctuated, and yet dimensional typefaces remain a constant staple on the typographic menu. Nevertheless, there are right and wrong ways to apply them. Shadow letters should not, as a rule, be used as body text for continuous reading (although this has been attempted), nor is it appropriate to use them indiscriminately. However, when it comes to conveying messages on a large scale, grabbing attention from long distances, or capturing the eye of someone in a fast-moving vehicle, few typographic styles are better suited—and there have always been many to choose from.

In this section, a series of historical specimens from Holland, Austria, Spain, Czechoslovakia, and the Soviet Union shows just how widespread the dimensional conceit was. Included are block letters, with and without serifs, that have architectonic shadows, drop shadows, back shadows, ghost shadows, airbrush shadows, shaded shadows, faint shadows, and monumental shadows. Each historical period had its own distinctive style, although most of the examples here are from the 1930s. There are Victorian shadows, Gothic shadows, and even some hybrid, more modern shadows. Some typefaces have a single shadow, others have multiple. An impression of mass and volume is the common denominator, and with each example the eye enjoys perceiving the illusion.

11
NÝ LIST ČESKOSLOV. KNIHTISKAŘŮ
ČNÍK TŘICÁTÝSEDMÝ • ČÍSLO 11 • R. 1930
VYCHÁZÍ MĚSÍČNĚ S PŘÍL. GRAF. PRACÍ
typografia

Erste, g
HUT
RESSE FÜR BRIEFE:
. SCHWAB.
WIEN, VI.
riahilferstrasse 71.
Ferdinan
Mariahi
EINGA
Herrn Jacob Isle

te Damen-Mode-
BRIK
Schwab
WIEN
VI. BEZ.
strasse No 71, I. Stock,
EN „HOTEL KUMMER"
KOLLERGERNGASSE No 3.
ADRESSE FÜR TELEGRAMME:
SCHWAB,
WIEN,
Mariahilferstrasse.
Wien, am

RADIO
BARCELONA
Año XI
Núm. 47
Barcelona, 23 Septiembre 193
40 cts.

MUNDO GRAFICO

Pro Estatuto Catalán

La manifestación celebrada el domingo último en Barcelona, al llegar ante el Palacio de la Generalidad

(Fot. Gaspar)

30 cts

TOS · RONQUERA · ASMA
BOMBONES
RIQUER
PRECIO: 0,95 CAJA
PUBLICOLOR BARCELONA

CNT
FAI
AIT

SP. AKC. CHEM. FABR.

DR. RATTNER

HUGO HAAS

v nejlepším českém filmu

Podle známé veselohry
Olgy Scheinpflugové.

Další obsazení: **LÍDA BAAROVÁ,**
Nedošínská, Pešek, Veleký, Marvan atd.

PREMIÉRA
od 3. března

KINO REPUBLIKA

Začátky o ¼4., ¼6., ¼8., 9½ hod. V neděli též o 11. hod. dopol. Předprodej od 10 do 12 hod. dopol.

DE RECLAME

OFFICIEEL ORGAAN VAN HET
GENOOTSCHAP VOOR RECLAME

8E JAARGANG No 6 JUNI 1929

VERSCHIJNT ELKE WEEK
1e JAARG. No. 32. 9 AUG. 1932
RED. & ADM. HOFWIJCKSTR. 9 DEN HAAG

. FUNKE

BRUX

ELLES

30%
Réduction spéciale
sur billets suisses
SUISSE

335. Cover of *Typografia* magazine, 1930 (Czechoslovakia).

336–37. Billhead for Ferdinand Schwab hat factory, 1891 (Austria).

338. Program cover for Radio Barcelona, 1933 (Spain).

339. Cover of *Mundo Grafico* magazine, *c.* 1935 (Spain).

340. Point-of-purchase candy display, 1930 (Spain).

341. Poster for the CNT FAI AIT trade union, 1938 (Spain).

342. Poster for Dr. Rattner (Poland).

343. Poster for the film *Okenko*, 1933 (Czechoslovakia).

344–45. Covers of *De Reclame* magazine, 1929 and 1932 (Netherlands).

346–47. Luggage label for Palace Hotel, 1932 (Belgium).

348. Advertisement for a travel sale, 1930s (Switzerland).

Annenberg, Maurice. *Type Foundries of America and Their Catalogs.* New Castle, Delaware: Oak Knoll Press, 1994.

Bruce's New York Type-Foundry. *Specimens of Printing Types.* New York: George Bruce's Son and Co., 1882.

Cabarga, Leslie. *Progressive German Graphics: 1900–1937.* San Francisco: Chronicle Books, 1994.

Carlyle, Paul, Guy Oring, and Herbert S. Richland. *Letters and Lettering.* New York and London: McGraw-Hill Book Company, 1943.

DeNoon, Christopher. *Posters of the WPA: 1935–1943.* Los Angeles: The Wheatley Press, 1987.

Fraser, James, and Steven Heller. *The Malik Verlag* (exhibition catalog). New York: Goethe House, 1983.

Heller, Steven, and Seymour Chwast. *Graphic Styles: From Victorian to Post-Modern.* New York: Harry N. Abrams, 1988.

Heller, Steven, and Louise Fili. *Deco Type: Stylish Alphabets of the '20s and '30s.* San Francisco: Chronicle Books, 1997.

Heller, Steven, and Louise Fili. *Typology: Type Design from the Victorian Era to the Digital Age.* San Francisco: Chronicle Books, 1999.

Hollis, Richard. *Graphic Design: A Concise History.* London and New York: Thames & Hudson, 2001.

Hutchings, R.S. *A Manual of Decorated Typefaces.* London: Cory, Adams and Mackay, 1965.

Kelly, Rob Roy. *American Wood Type: 1828–1900: Notes on the Evolution of Decorated and Large Types.* New York: Da Capo Press, 1969.

Lewis, John. *The Twentieth Century Book: Its Illustration and Design.* London: Studio Vista Limited, 1967.

Lewis, John. *Printed Ephemera: The Changing Uses of Type and Letterforms in English and American Printing.* Woodbridge, Suffolk: The Antique Collectors Club, 1990.

Lista, Giovanni. *Le Livre Futuriste: De la libération du mot au poème tactile.* Modena: Panini, 1984.

McLean, Ruari. *Victorian Book Design and Colour Printing.* London: Faber & Faber, 1963. Enlarged edition, 1972.

McLean, Ruari. *Pictorial Alphabets.* London: Studio Vista, 1969.

Sembach, Klaus-Jürgen. *Style 1930: Elegance and Sophistication in Architecture, Design, Fashion, Graphics, and Photography.* New York: Universe Books, 1971.

Shriften Atlas. H. Berthold. Vienna, 1914.

Spécimen Général. Fonderies Deberny et Peignot. Paris, 1926.

Wood Letter. Stephenson, Blake, & Co., Ltd. Sheffield, 1939.

MUCH GRATITUDE GOES TO LUCAS DIETRICH, our main editor, and Adélia Sabatini at Thames & Hudson for their continued enthusiastic support of *Shadow Type* and the earlier *Scripts* book.

Thanks to Spencer Charles of Louise Fili Ltd for his excellent work on the layouts and cover, and to Kelly Thorn for her design assistance.

The book's content is entirely from our own collections, but these would not be possible without the tips from dealers and friends, and friends who are dealers.

Finally, thank you to Irving Oaklander, bookseller, who passed away in 2012, and who supplied us with incredible typographic riches.

S.H. & L.F.

FIN